The Intelligent Homeowner

BRYAN CRABTREE

BRYAN CRABTREE

THE INTELLIGENT HOMEOWNER

Copyright © 2018 BRYAN CRABTREE & TALK40.COM

All rights reserved.

ISBN:1720462453

ISBN-13:9781720462453

DEDICATION

This book is dedicated to the homeowner. For two decades I've participated in an industry that is scandalous, ruthless, and abusive to homeowners. Real estate is a wonderful asset and a path to wealth, but it can be a recipe for disaster if you don't avoid the sharks who try to take a bite out of your financial wellbeing.

THE INTELLIGENT HOMEOWNER

CONTENTS

	Introduction	8
1	Buy when the market needs buyers	11
2	Sell when the market needs sellers	16
3	How to sell a home for more money than it's worth	26
4	Investing in land	38
5	Working with Realtors and agents.	41
6	An industry full of frauds	46
7	Finding the best deals	58
8	The philosophy of home pricing	67
9	Emotion will cost you	71

10	Private money loans	78
11	Negotiation	82
12	Homeowners' Associations	98
13	Paying off your primary home	109
14	Conclusion	115

INTRODUCTION

As stated in my previous book, I don't like long introductions. Normally I start reading chapter 1 when I pick up a book.

Here's my short introduction: this book is for every person who wants to make money in real estate ownership. That's why call it the intelligent homeowner. This is not about the real estate industry.

If you're in our industry, and this book offends you, I'm not interested in your opinion. Don't 'beat up on me' because I call out our industry for how it disadvantages and abuses homeowners across this country.

This book is for my readers, American consumers, my clients, and customers. It is the result of 20 years of watching so-called real estate professionals, with limited knowledge and ability, mislead and embarrass our industry.

This book has one purpose: to help readers avoid incompetent and dangerous housing-industry workers while creating financial freedom and wealth in their lives.

1 Buy when the market needs buyers

The name of this chapter may seem like an obvious statement. However, the best real estate advice you'll ever hear is that you should always "buy when the market needs buyers and sell when the market needs sellers." There is no seminar, no book, no expert, nor any guidance that is evermore instructive to success than this principle of real estate investing.

A wise and rich real estate investor told me early in my career that it's always best to buy when there's 'blood on the streets.' Little did I know that a decade later we would endure the worst real estate crisis in American history.

From 2011 to 2013, the national housing industry became one big going out of business sale. In recent years, a number of major retailers have also gone bust: Gander Mountain, Toys "R" Us, Circuit City, and others. These liquidation sales are a result of complete failure, usually a chapter 7 bankruptcy.

The housing crash from 2008 to 2012 was no different. It was one big chapter 7 bankruptcy sale. Early in the sale, prices fell 10 to 15%. While it was a discount compared to previous prices, it was no deal. It was similar to retailers whose pricing was likely too high, keeping their sales low and driving them into bankruptcy.

By 2011, the real estate market throughout our nation resembled the last couple of weeks of a chapter 7 bankruptcy going out of business sale. Prices were reduced 75 to 80% in some markets. In the best markets we saw prices cut in half.

Conventional wisdom instructs most people to avoid these times out of fear. By contrast, this is when smart investors rush in with capital and buy everything they can.

Using just the cash from my real estate brokerage income, my wife and I purchased several properties during the housing crash. We purchased one for $38,000 that had sold just a couple of years earlier for $155,000. It was a condo, in a community without conventional or government approval for lending. In other words, no bank would lend money on this condo. As a result, there were no buyers as even many cash buyers were equally afraid of it. Not me!

Since no one wanted to buy it, it obviously had to be a great deal. This means that I would have no competition in purchasing it and negotiating much better terms. I also calculated that with the current rental rate similar condominiums were achieving, even if the property had zero value in the future I would have all of my money back in about five years simply by collecting rent. We paid cash so there was no mortgage.

As of this writing, that property has quadrupled in value in seven years. I bought when the market needed buyers and I just listed the property for sale since the market needs sellers now. We'll talk about this concept in the next chapter.

We bought multiple properties that year and have had a similar experience with all of them. We repeated this cycle from 2011 all the way through 2016. By that point the market had become hot again. The deals were beginning to evaporate and prices were noticeably rising. We shifted our model to focus only on distressed properties. What came next?

Even in the hot and rising market of the last couple of years it is still a distressed situation. There are hundreds of thousands of properties nationwide stuck on banks' balance sheets that were part of the toxic loan crisis that created the last housing crash. As a result of the sloppy paperwork of the early 21st-century housing boom and the rapid failure of many banks, some homeowners haven't made mortgage payments in four, five, even six years as those homes have been tied up in litigation.

Due to the sloppiness of many of these banks, they have lost nearly all favor in the judicial system and have been fined heavily for their illicit activity by the federal government. This means that major mortgage servicing companies struggle to foreclose on properties and subsequently need to evict the occupants. These mortgage companies and banks struggle now with a greater deal of judicial scrutiny.

Because of this, many of these foreclosures, still owned by banks, are being liquidated to cash purchasers on no contingency contracts at a substantial discount. These mortgage companies are fearful of the risk and public relations crisis each time they have to evict a holdover tenant or former homeowner who has been foreclosed. This creates opportunity for people like me and maybe you!

Banks are incompetent in a general sense. They read spreadsheets and columns but they don't really know how to predict human behavior in the housing business. This is why they had so much trouble processing all their foreclosures because they use a robotic approach to real human issues and challenges.

Most of the properties we purchased, renovated, and flipped were owner-occupied at the time of the foreclosure. However, out of 20 or more investment flips only one was occupied at the time of our purchase. In that scenario, it was a holdover tenant and we began collecting rent until she could find suitable replacement housing. Banks find a different experience because they don't treat these people as humans. They are just part of a numbers-game.

The market changed on the banks and they didn't even realize it. In processing foreclosures in an economy that's gotten much better, most of these foreclosed homeowners were simply seeing how long they could live in their home for free and just taking their foreclosure as a cue to move.

We recently purchased a property for $135,000 near Atlanta, invested about $15,000 (including closing costs and repairs) and sold it for $195,000 two months later. We paid the buyer's agent a 3% commission. You can do the math on that one. Banks frequently leave money on the table due to their incompetent service process and outsourcing.

While the market was very strong during this transaction, we discovered a niche in the market that was appealing to the mortgage company that sold us this home. They want cash purchasers, who will agree not to do an inspection and will close in less than 30 days.

Most buyers are afraid to buy a home without an inspection. It's always amazed me that buyers receiving a $30,000 discount on a property worry they might have $5-$10,000 in hidden damage. Who cares?

If someone offered you a bag containing 200 hundred-dollar bills ($20,000), would you ask them if it's counterfeit or just simply take the bag? Most people would start asking questions. I'd take the damn bag and figure out if it's counterfeit later. While this may be an overly simplistic scenario, I see 'wanna-be' home investors and/or homebuyers do this consistently.

They stand in front of a wonderful opportunity, where they can earn substantial instant equity and systematically talk themselves and the seller out of the deal. This usually comes in the form of being too difficult and picky. 'Beggars can't be choosers' applies here.

In the hottest and weakest of markets, you can apply the scenario 'buy when the market needs buyers.' You simply have to be looking for the segments of the market that are the least popular, with the most distress or at least the least trendy.

When no one wants to buy condos, buy condos. When everyone is buying the hottest, most exciting new neighborhood, don't. Trends don't last. Great locations do. Don't follow the sheep and buy where everyone else is. You'll never make money in real estate doing it that way. Buy in the best locations and rehab the home(s).

The next big problem that most homeowners and investors have is timing the sale of their property. There are only two points in your life where most people sell a piece of real estate: When you want to and when you need to.

Newsflash: neither of those matter to the market.

The time to sell is always when the market needs sellers. So, how do you determine when that is? That is our next chapter.

2 SELL WHEN THE MARKET NEEDS SELLERS

For your benefit, I want to repeat the second opening sentence of the last chapter: "The best real estate advice you will ever hear is that you should always buy when the market needs buyers and sell when the market needs sellers."

I've outlined how to look for market scenarios that present the best opportunity to buy. One thing I forgot to mention, but is highly appropriate here, is that you make all of your money in real estate when you buy. You lose money when you sell.

Considering that I've made most of my real estate brokerage income from helping people sell homes, it may be shocking that I made most of my money at the point where people are losing money. That's at least how it appears on the surface. In reality, my job (as a real estate broker) is to help people mitigate their losses as a seller and maximize the equity they tap out of their property.

The biggest loss I've ever suffered on a piece of real estate was the time I purchased a primary residence on the water, in a hot neighborhood, at the top of the market, and in premium condition. Don't get me wrong. It was the dream house. It was magnificent and I don't necessarily regret buying it because I got to enjoy it for six years before we sold it. That said, I'll never do that again.

My model has always been to buy the ugliest house in the neighborhood and, when possible, the cheapest. If you're moving into a neighborhood full of million-dollar homes, the best home to buy is the 'dog' down the street that everyone hates that is several hundred thousand dollars cheaper. Yes, you may be in the most embarrassing home in the neighborhood. However, you'll be the least embarrassed of your bottom line when you sell it.

It's always easier to sell the cheapest home in the neighborhood as opposed to the most expensive. It's also easier to negotiate a better deal on a home no one wants (because it's ugly) and then fix it yourself. Many people are too overwhelmed or proud to buy an ugly home, interview contractors, and hire one to fully renovate it. Instead, they buy the nicest home they can find at the most premium price possible and then beat the crap out of it over the next 5 to 10 years. Then, they expect the same premium for a used, abused home. It doesn't work that way.

That's when I show up. They're ready to sell it and their mindset is still stuck in the day they decided to purchase it. Of course a ten-year old home is likely missing the latest colors, the most exciting new appliances, the most popular granite, and all of the latest technology. However, homes are just like cars. The most technologically advanced (overpriced) car today is just an old used car five years from now. Most people get emotionally attached to all of these exceptional features and justify overpaying for them by convincing themselves they will get an even bigger return when they sell it. Honestly, the real estate community (especially agents) preys on this ignorance. Agents encourage it, repeat it, and convince these homebuyers (now my seller-clients) that this is true.

It isn't.

I love putting 'lipstick on pigs.' Buying an ugly house, planning a renovation, and executing a vision is not only fun but can also be highly rewarding from a financial perspective. I've never understood why a seller expects to get top market value for a home, especially under the circumstances I described above, without doing significant renovations or upgrades. Sometimes they simply don't have the money to do it. Nonetheless, buyers tend to buy the most upgraded homes at the most premium prices regardless of what I suggest in this book.

The point here is that I always buy the worst home in the neighborhood, if I can find it. Generally, I'm only selling one of the best homes in the neighborhood. This means I go for the cheapest, and I plan to sell the highest. This ties back to my point that you make almost all of your money when you buy. I am always selling the home that no one should buy and buying a home no one wants to buy.

No matter how many radio shows I do or how many people I tell, I will never impact even 1% of the people who will buy and sell homes incorrectly this year. They will consistently hire the real estate companies with the worst gimmicks and scams, align themselves with the people who tell them what they want to hear, and generally ignore advice that suggests they put a little sweat equity into a home in order to insulate themselves from losing money and potentially set themselves up to make a ton of money.

Some people will even sell their home via the latest fad of "we buy it" brokerages. These companies prey on ignorance and offer to help sellers avoid showings, repairs, and other home-selling preparations. My research has proven that the cost for this 'convenience' is 25-28% of your equity. On the average home of $300,000, that's $75,000+. No thanks! I'll go through the hassles of showing and selling for that kind of money!

Since the theme of this chapter is 'Sell when the market needs sellers,' how do you determine when that is?

There are several indicators, but the best indicator is when homes on your street (or at least in your community) are selling in a few days with multiple offers and frequently over list price. This may come as a shock but those conditions generally only last four months to a couple of years every two decades or so.

This book is being written in 2018 and the last time we saw multiple offers and sales over list price the way we are seeing them now was in 2005. That's 13 years ago!

But, what do you do if you don't want to sell your primary residence now but you're seeing these conditions? Wait 13 years! It's really that simple.

Most sellers sell a home when they want to or when they need to. Sometimes needing to sell a home is not controllable. People lose their jobs, become sick, buy too much home in the first place, or have other distresses.

While the mortgage and real estate industry wants you to buy a home with a monthly payment equivalent to roughly 50% of your entire household income, I think that is disgusting. I never recommend under any circumstances that an individual or family spend more than 30% of their gross income on their housing payment. In fact, I think 25% is even safer. They know that a 50% loan-to-value necessitates their overpriced mortgage protection insurance and a few egregious late fees along the journey of repaying their loan. Homeowners rarely factor in these hidden costs when considering real estate.

The typical family with two incomes, 2.3 kids, and 1.5 dogs can sustain the loss of one income if their mortgage payment is 25% of their total household income when they purchase. In other words, if one spouse loses their job, then for that unemployment period, their mortgage may be 50% of their household income. However, a household with the discipline to buy far less home than they can afford is also likely to be saving money at a faster rate due to lower mortgage payments. In this scenario, this job loss is not a substantial threat to your financial security. It's simply a setback to your pace of savings. Having a nice home AND money in the bank are two related, key ingredients to financial freedom.

Families who use both of their incomes to qualify for a mortgage that equates to upwards of 50% of their household income are playing financial, Russian roulette. They are staking their entire financial future on both of them keeping their jobs and income level, without disruption. If they are accurate, their lifestyle will be ahead of other people in their income demographics. If they are wrong, they will be on the brink of bankruptcy.

Being able to buy when the market needs buyers and sell when the market needs sellers requires you to see a home, not as an extension of you, but as a tool to a successful life. This means that sometimes you have to sell a home sooner than you may wish. At times you may have to delay an upgrade of that home longer than you wish. In reality, if you are confident that your company will be transferring you to a new marketplace in the next three to five years, and your neighbors are seeing multiple offers over list price, you should sell now.

Building real estate wealth and controlling the timing and

convenience of when you buy and sell a home are not usually in tandem.

Many people follow up by asking "what will I do about housing if I sell it now (too soon)?" You'll rent. History tells us that when the market is on fire and people are paying over full price, it will likely peak and correct in the near future. Wouldn't it be great to sell at the top, rent for a little while, and buy at the new bottom?

I understand how inconvenient that would be to your family. It's nearly as inconvenient as having to go to work every day for eight or more hours to actually pay for a home. With sacrifice and work comes money and freedom!

However, if you don't plan to leave the city and you're happy with your current home, then why move? Let's say that you will be an empty-nester in three to five years, and your kids will be gone. You're thinking that you probably won't need that six-bedroom house in the suburbs by that point, right? But homes are selling rapidly and for over full-price and you're thinking about selling. Why?

You still have your kids living with you in a house that you previously decided fits the needs for the size of your family and financial situation. You don't need to sell it for the next three to five years. Let's play this forward. In fact, in three to five years, your kids are gone to college, you no longer need a home this large, and the market has crashed again. Most people beat themselves up wishing they had sold the home. Why?

In this scenario, you simply hold the home until the market needs sellers again and then you sell. At times, it's as if we believe the market is so high that this will never end. At other times we seem to react as if the market is so soft it'll never be good again. Yet, history tells us this is simply not true.

Selling a home should never be because you 'want to' or 'need to.' It doesn't matter whether it's an investment, second home, or primary residence, you sell it when it makes sense for your family and the market is at the hottest. If the market is hot and it doesn't make sense, don't sell it. By contrast, if it does make sense to sell it but the market is soft, don't sell it. Wait until the market gets hot again.

The reason most people can't do this is because they bought more home than they can truly afford. By the time you're 50, regardless of the age of your children, you should consider whether you have a financial situation that will allow you to continue to afford this home in retirement should you be stuck with it for longer than you plan. Many people get to retirement, on a reduced income and the reality that the monster home they own is no longer affordable. This is why my advice to spend no more than 25% of your household's gross income on housing eliminates all of these issues.

Most people can't time the market because they don't make the proper financial decisions when entering homeownership.

Here's another shocking aspect of home buying and selling. In the real estate industry, we are notorious for calling a primary residence "an investment." A primary residence is NOT an investment. It's a liability.

In fact, if your job frequently transfers you from one city to another, without a relocation buyout package, then homeownership might not even be the best idea for your family.

I do not believe in real estate ownership for speculative reasons. What I mean by this is that I find no personal value in the appreciation of homes. Don't get me wrong. I love the fact that homes appreciate consistently and steadily decade by decade. However, I no longer factor this in to my investment strategy. Why? Remember 2008-2011?

If the market is hot, I buy very little. If the market is very cold, I buy a lot. Because this is in direct contrast with most of America, I can assume that my homes will always be worth at least what I paid for them. I assume nothing more and I suppose the potential for a little less.

Since those are my assumptions, and they are generally the exact opposite assumptions that most people in America make about housing, then what is the benefit of homeownership?

There are two benefits: First, as investments, there is cash flow from rental income. Second, as a primary residence, there is ego.

Some individuals are bothered by the fact I call it ego. Ego is not a bad thing, but it can be. Ego speaks to self-esteem and self-importance.

Owning my home is more prestigious. Owning my home gives me more control. Owning my home gives me more stability. If I feel a sense of accomplishment and prestige, garner more control, and realize more stability from homeownership (primary residence only), then statistics show my family will realize more success as a result. No landlord can sell the home and force me to move. My children are not forced to move at times that can be the most sensitive to their development. Stability and its resulting rhythm are great for spouses and their children.

However, if my career or other life circumstances cause me to move more frequently, I lose control of that stability. The prestige and control of homeownership then gets offset by the ebbs and flows of market appreciation and depreciation. I lose control of when to sell and when to buy. The ego of homeownership, in these circumstances, is negated by the reality of it being a liability.

This chapter was to instruct you on how to sell when the market needs sellers and how to time your financial life to make that possible. In reality, this chapter was more about buying at the right time for the right price and structuring your financial picture to allow success with your housing purchases/investments.

The critical factor to success in housing is to never spend more than 25-30% of your household income on a housing payment. A primary residence is a liability not an investment. The only benefit of ownership, other than a place to live, is cash flow.

With these principles in mind, you almost can't fail. Avoid these principles, and you'll be like the rest of America: one disaster away from financial calamity or bankruptcy.

Now that I have described how/when to properly buy and sell real estate, time the market, and maximize your equity, there's one more key factor: marketing.

How do you sell a home for even more money than it's worth (on paper)?

THE INTELLIGENT HOMEOWNER

3 How to sell a home for more money than it's worth.

The original title of this chapter was 'Marketing.' But, then I would sound like every other 'know-it-all' real estate agent who has the best marketing, is 'number one in their market,' and knows everything about everything.

You're reading this book because you want to know more than average.

Here's the reality: real estate people suck. Most of them got into the business because they saw how much their real estate agent made on the purchase or sale of a home and thought that they could replace their $50,000 salary with three or four sales the year. That thought process is about as stupid as opening up a car lot thinking if you can just sell four or five Lamborghinis per year at a $50,000 profit each you'll do great.

The truth is that most companies who sell Lamborghinis lose money selling Lamborghinis. They make money on everything else. The purpose of selling the Lamborghinis is to get people to come to their car lot out of curiosity for $350,000 sports car in the hope of them driving off the lot in a $40-80,000 car. The real money was made on the document preparation fees, the factory kickback, and points paid to the dealership by the bank and committed to the loan or lease.

Housing is no different. Most real estate agents are part-time. The average real estate agent in Metro Atlanta, where I'm based, sells about two homes per year. That's a fact! Based on average sales prices they're bringing in a whopping $14,000 per year as so-called experts in real estate. I wouldn't even call that a hobby: I'd call it embarrassing. By the time they pay their broker about half of their commission (including fees and dues), they're paying taxes on $7000 in net income. Welcome to poverty!

The reality is that most people with real estate licenses have them to sell or buy their own real estate and to pick up some tax benefits along the way. I would estimate that roughly 95% of all real estate agents fall into this category I just described.

This means that if you call 20 real estate agents, the odds are that 19 of them are incompetent, unqualified, and incapable of serving your needs. Their only skill is convincing you they know what they're doing. A rare few of us are at the PhD level of real estate. That means less than 5% of agents have the equivalent of a doctorate or master's degree. Most agents are still at the kindergarten level.

Dealing with the real estate industry is an absolute necessity for any home buyer or seller. It's possible to buy dozens of homes per year and never talk to a real estate agent. However, at some point, if you choose to sell one of those homes or properties, you're not going to bypass this kindergarten of so-called professionals and simultaneously get the most money for your home.

The research (from Collateral Analytics Research) shows that attempting to sell For Sale By Owner (FSBO) is a guaranteed loss of 13% of your home's equity. In other words, it's insane! You will ALWAYS leave money on the table as a FSBO, verses listing with a quality agent.

The vast majority of real estate agents are driven by money. They're not driven by righteousness, ethics, morality, or (as they frequently and disgustingly state) their love for working with people. That's all bull sh**. We're all driven by money.

Some of us believe that we make more money than we could possibly imagine by conducting daily activities that lead to more clients thus leading to more sales. My philosophy has always been that if I help my clients accomplish what they wish to do while performing for them in the same manner for which I would conduct my own personal deals, then I'll get more referrals, more business, and make more money. Loosely translated, don't screw people over, treat them right, and work hard for them then and you'll make even more money than those who don't follow these guidelines.

Sadly, most agents see dollar signs, not you.

Now that we've established the truth that most every professional in the real estate business is out for money, you have to guard yours. If you don't, they'll take it. The more you trust people in the real estate and mortgage industry the more you're going to lose. After all, the more you spend the more we make.

This is not to say that you can't hire a great real estate agent who will serve your best interests and at the same time make great money. This is simply to say that <u>most</u> real estate agents serve only their interests without any concern for yours.

Here's how the intelligent homeowner mitigates these always competing circumstances. First, when you need to sell property you have an inherent conflict of interest with everyone in the real estate industry including the buyers. You desire the absolute most money with the fewest costs. That is in conflict with both buyers and agents alike.

When most sellers decide to sell, their first concern is the real estate commission. This is like saying "I really want to buy a NEW Porsche 911 Turbo, but I only want to pay $95,000 for it." Considering that the 911 Turbo is $200,000+, I'd call this delusional.

Most sellers make this the key ingredient in selecting an agent: commission rate. But, what I say next may shock you. You should always attempt to negotiate commission. Why would I tell you that given that that is my lifeblood?

I want you to attempt to negotiate my commission, because I want you to see how I fight for my money. If a real estate agent comes to your home, you attempt to negotiate commission and within five minutes you can get them to drop their fee by 1% or more, run! If they won't even fight for their own money they're sure as hell not going to fight for yours. Any real estate agent willing to drop their fee before they meet with you or quickly in the discussion will also disadvantage you in every negotiation throughout the process.

If you want the most successful and capable real estate agent to help you maximize your equity, you should always attempt to negotiate the commission but never expect to actually succeed. You will never find the best people willing to cut their fees just like you won't find that new 911 Turbo for $95,000.

Disclaimer: I charge 5 to 10% depending on the home or property I'm selling. Don't assume the market is a set percentage. It's not. However, if an agent quotes you a fee and then shows a willingness to negotiate it, integrity is missing. I sometimes offer lower fees on hotter houses right up front, but once I quote it, it's not negotiable.

Many home sellers have convinced themselves they are being clever by negotiating the fee. The agents who accept this negotiation and succumb (offering a lower fee) are desperate. They also become resentful. You may find this hard to believe, but they actually sometimes negotiate against their clients as a punitive measure for how harshly the seller/owner negotiated with them.

You need a real estate advocate, not an enemy.

The other problem that homeowners have when selling property is that they hire an agent and then command them to do certain mundane tasks that are proven to be ineffective when selling homes. This usually results from a homeowner choosing the wrong agent in the first place.

I generally tell people that if you expect me to do an agent open house (caravan) or a community open house, as an example, I am not the right agent for you. I'm simply not going to be doing those things because they are a complete waste of time and are generally an invitation for the worst real estate agents with no clients and neighbors with no interest in purchasing to visit the home. I frequently reply to such requests by outlining the fact that for the $300 I would spend feeding a bunch of real estate agents who have no buyers (or virtually none), I could use Google and Bing to identify the name, email address, and phone number of 30 people who have some level of interest in the home (your home) I'm trying to sell.

It amazes me that someone will go online on a site like Zillow or (our site) TheRealEstateExperts.com, shop for a home, save the properties they like, and eliminate the ones they don't, all from the comfort of their home, somehow suspect that inviting neighbors and real estate agents to an open house is going to do anything positive for their home selling experience.

Over 60% of real estate searches are on a smart phone. Over 94% of homebuyers find their home online. Less than 1% found a home visiting an open house. If you could buy a lottery ticket with 94% odds of winning verses one with 1% odds of winning, which ticket would you buy?

It's akin to being stuck in 1995 and 2019 at the same time. Having one foot stuck in the past while having another in the present or future is never a good idea in business.

The reason that so many people are sold on the idea of traditional real estate marketing such as open houses, postcards, brochures, and other print collateral is that real estate agents generally don't know anything about marketing. Since they know very little and can explain virtually nothing, they peddle useless ideas that can be seen (visually) and recognized as marketing. Online marketing is not easy to see in a vacuum for a seller marketing-presentation and therefore most agents fail to embrace it and the sales power it offers.

Let's say that my job is to sell multi-million-dollar yachts to wealthy billionaires. Doing a real estate open house is akin to standing outside of a Walmart to meet billionaires who may want to buy a yacht. Everyone wants the yacht, but NO ONE can afford it.

However, I can certainly be seen talking to 100 people outside of Walmart about my multi-million-dollar yachts to prove that I'm making a solid, noticeable effort. That's what the real estate community does to home sellers. "Look how hard Crabtree is working outside of Wal-Mart to sell that million dollar yacht. He's such a great agent!" No, that would make me an idiotic agent if I did that.

Regretfully, a lot of sellers say to me about these agents "they're really hard workers." I have a different word for these agents: scammers.

If I want to sell my multi-million-dollar yachts, then I've got to find a gathering of CEOs from Fortune 500 companies. The likelihood is that no one's going to see me doing that. Google and Bing are the same way. Every home we list has a likely buyer profile. Each price point generally coincides with an income range, proximity to workplace, churches, schools, and activities. By identifying those lifestyle choices that are most associated with an individual home or property we are then able to target those specific people for that specific home.

The boring techniques in the online marketplace work! We can provide in-depth analytics and results data, but you can't physically see me sweating in the heat putting up useless open house signs. Sorry!

I do want to highlight what an intelligent homeowner should seek in a real estate professional. The professional should outline a marketing plan that's easy to understand, not highly technical, and presented with a high level of confidence, accountability, and proven results. They should be able to suggest how you will hold them accountable along with results and testimonials from past clients to illustrate their plan's effectiveness. But what does this all mean?

As an example, our plan on properties includes staging the property at some level, taking professional photographs, and then launching the marketing using enhanced online systems (not just pressing enter on a keyboard). In this new rapid, digital-age, most homeowners and agents want to list the property, put it on the market the next day, and have it sold in 24 hours. That's a disastrous plan.

We like to first put a sign in the yard, creating urgency while we're getting the photography and staging completed. Then once the property is in the multiple listing service (MLS), it has a complete marketing presentation. This means having all of the photos and materials online when we launch the marketing.

Have you ever seen an automobile company launch a new vehicle without providing a picture and an elaborate description of how their new car model is the latest and greatest of all of the competitors on the market? Usually, homes cost far more than cars yet our industry does a terrible job with presentation.

Automobile companies release coming soon ads and images, followed by a launch presentation and description well before you can actually buy the car. Once they formally add it as a model on their website, they allow you to sell everything possibly available in terms of features. They only do this once they can bind you to a sale and the car is in production or on the car lot.

In hot markets, most real estate agents don't understand how to maximize equity for home sellers. If a full price offer comes in the first 24 hours, conventional wisdom is to take that offer. I think it's a bad idea to ever sell a property in the first four to five days it's listed.

I recently had a home that was listed above market value in metro Atlanta and we had 20 showings scheduled through the first week. We had a full price offer on day one and I recommend that we wait five days until we accept the offer. By the time those five days had passed we had 10 offers and accepted one with a very strong financing contingency at 11% over our list price.

When I see homes that sell at or near full price in one to three days on the market, I know one thing about that marketing process: it was wrong. Likely, the seller left money on the table and gave it to the buyer because of their weak and incompetent real estate agent.

Over my 20 years in the real estate business I've encountered dozens of sellers who have fired their agent over the handling of multiple offers. Many agents are so sanctimonious that they believe that it is incumbent upon the seller to accept the first full price offer they receive. This is a combination of giving loyalty to the wrong people, laziness, and incompetence.

As an agent, dealing with a home that has 10 offers in the period of one week is as much work as selling three or four houses. Remember, I admitted that I'm in this business for money. However, I also told you that I believe in doing for my sellers what I would do for myself as an intelligent homeowner.

Since this is not only about my seller's money but also about my commission, with 10 offers, I want to be 100% certain that the deal we ratify will close. This means that it's in our mutual best interest to vet each purchaser's ability to close and factor that into the decision. In some instances, this means taking, not the highest offer, but the one we trust the most.

Inexperienced agents frequently miss the fact that multiple offer situations bring out the worst from buyers' agents and their clients. Many simply offer pie-in-the-sky numbers to get a seller to accept the deal. In most cases they have no ability to close at that price or have no intention of actually paying. They'll use the appraisal, financing, and other contingencies to renegotiate the price once all of the other buyers are removed from the equation. Once a seller agrees to a contract in a multiple offer situation, they lose most of the leverage and cede it to the buyer.

 You hire a solid agent because you want them to create a bidding war for your property and at times earn you more money than what you're even paying them in the commission. In the absence of that most desired scenario, you then want an agent who has the ability to quickly alter their marketing plan or strategy to match the feedback from the showings and sell it quickly.

 Many sellers come to this process with an arrogance that they've sold many homes in their lives (usually over 20-30 years) and thus know more than most real estate agents. This may actually be true. However, an intelligent homeowner should become very skilled at finding and using the financial experts with which they partner. The intelligent homeowner should always hire someone who knows far more about their desired financial goals (within their industry) than they do.

 If you feel empowered because you know more than your real estate agent, financial advisor, insurance agent, auto salesperson, or other financial provider you're surrounding yourself with the wrong people who will steer you in a dangerous direction. You must surround yourself with people you can trust.

 I'm not advocating blind trust here; I'm simply saying find people whom you believe will attempt to serve your best interest at the same time they serve their own. That's the best you can hope for across the financial-sales spectrum.

You should judge us by how we react to the challenges you forge against our recommendations and opinions. You should not judge professionals if they push back on some of your opinions. In fact, I generally get very nervous about professionals/advisors who agree with most everything I say (outside of the real estate industry in my own personal life). This is the oldest trick in the book and most people fall for it. I don't like human-parrots. They are the most destructive to all of us because they encourage us to believe what's wrong is right (so we'll like and hire them).

The best way an advisor can earn my trust and respect is to be willing to challenge me on multiple issues throughout our relationship. This allows me the opportunity to see that instead of being a salesperson they're trying to be an advisor. Most people act in the opposite way to what I'm describing here. The best salesperson or advisor challenges your/my viewpoint, so you/me are well informed.

Debates are some of the best ways for partners to make the best decisions. Your real estate agent and you, the intelligent homeowner, are partners at least for a short period of time. It's a team effort. The best way to develop the best strategy is to hire someone who can speak to your specific objections and concerns while respecting your opinion. This is generally a God-given talent not easily learned.

There are very few real estate agents who can perform in this sort of environment without being pushy and obnoxious.

I'm not giving you a lot of steps to take in this chapter about how to earn the most money for your home. I'm only giving you what you need to know. The best real estate agents are worth their weight in goal for taking actual steps that result in more dollars to you.

- If you hire an agent that will negotiate their own fee, they will easily give up a lot of your money too.
- If you hire an agent that agrees with everything you say, they are not trying to help you obtain what you want. They're a parrot. They are simply trying to earn a quick commission at your expense.
- If you hire a cheap agent, you'll have virtually no chance of a bidding war on your home or negotiated terms that give you leverage instead of the buyer. Ceding leverage costs you real money. You may save a point toward a commission but give up several points in equity.
- The best way to get the most money for your home is a marketing strategy that is patient and has an opportunity to create a bidding war.
- Unless you are selling 20 or 30 homes per year you should never hire a real estate agent who does not know significantly more than you do about marketing and selling homes in the present market.
- It is usually not a good idea to accept an offer/contract in the first five days of your home-marketing.
- The best financial advisors will challenge you when they think you are making a bad decision. They won't be silent, so don't be offended.

I kept these bullet points simple because these are the mistakes that cost millions of homeowners billions of dollars per year.

We'll talk more about components of the home selling scams of the 21st century later in the book. Next, let's get into investing in real estate.

4 INVESTING IN LAND

Land is a speculative investment in most cases. Unless you can rent your land, ownership is a liability. There are very few exceptions for the vast majority of investors.

Earlier, I stated that investing in real estate is generally for the purpose of cash flow or ego. Land is rarely the former. In many cases, ego drives this 'investment.'

However, there are times when taking on the liability of land makes financial sense. First, if you have a lot of cash and residual cash flow to pay the taxes, land banking can be extremely profitable over the long run.

For instance, if Walmart just purchased a huge tract of land and you have a chance to buy a tract 100 yards away, that has historically been a real estate slam-dunk. The inherent risk is that Walmart never builds its retail center and thus you lose money. On the other hand, you may see your land quadruple in value in a very short period of time. Remember, I'm not big on speculation of value so the end-game for me on land-banking would be to build a cash-flow positive building on it.

Land-banking is educated blackjack. Better put, you become the house and the market becomes the player. In blackjack, the odds favor the house by about 3%. Over time, and with a lot of cash on hand, you'll make a lot of money.

The problem most land investors make is that they create debt to buy land. If anything goes wrong they lose a ton of money. If everything goes right, they make a little money having most of their profits negated by the interest carry it takes to develop and transition the land into a profitable project.

Investing in land is almost always for people who have a lot of cash, risk tolerance, and patience.

The only benefit to a piece of land for the intelligent homeowner is when it's a once-in-a-lifetime opportunity. I recently had a discussion with a friend of mine about a residential property he was purchasing on a historical waterway in a very popular community.

I suggested that I thought his emotional attachment to this area was clouding his judgment. He immediately pushed back and showed how it could be developed commercially or into townhomes. He told me "if we can get either approved, we can subdivide the land and sell one of the lots for 75% of what we paid for the whole parcel." He then told me there were three options with this land, this was also a once-in-a-lifetime opportunity because in 20 years only two lots on this street had been available for sale. I retracted my previous comments as it became clear he had multiple exit and profit strategies all of which made sense.

The reality is that while he was buying this land in an area where he had a deep emotional attachment he had developed contingency plans for how to make money with the property. He sourced other partners with substantial cash to help him purchase it. One of his partners is an engineer with substantial experience in these types of situations. He found the opportunity, and he found people with money to pay for it.

Finding the deals is as valuable as having all the money. Most people with a ton of money have a hard time finding the best deals and places to invest it. The best way to invest in real estate with no money is to become really good at finding deals. I have always found that the money tends to show up if you develop that single talent.

The intelligent homeowner may be working in a similar area to what I've described above for a unique piece of property to build a primary residence. If, as I described in the earlier chapters, their mortgage debt to income ratio on their current primary home is under 25%, they can both qualify and accept some risk on a once-in-a-lifetime opportunity. If half of their monthly income is going to a mortgage, they wouldn't be wise to either create a new one to purchase land or even pay cash for it.

Land is incredibly risky. Because of the risk factor, it also can produce exponential returns. Investing in land is not for the faint of heart and generally not for anyone who doesn't have a lot of cash.

Creating cash flow is the best avenue for financial freedom and longevity in real estate investing. Therefore, land isn't usually a good idea.

5 Working with Realtors and Agents

I was always told that if you can't say something good about someone then don't say anything at all. This chapter flies in the face of those instructions.

The main reason I'm in the real estate industry is because my early, adult experiences with real estate agents were deplorable. I found them disinterested in my needs, let alone my wants. They were dismissive of my concerns and they couldn't give a damn about my financial future. As a 19-year-old first-time homebuyer, and for my next couple of deals, I felt abused by the real estate industry.

Maybe I'm wrong, but I believe most intelligent homeowners feel that the real estate industry is full of scam artists. I'm in the industry, so I know that it is.

The gimmicks and/or scams in our industry are endless. There are agents that promise to buy your home if they can't sell it. We've recently seen companies who claim to buy your next home, so you can move in while they sell your present home. These instant-gratification conveniences all equal one thing: stealing your equity and financial freedom. What do you do if the market takes a downturn and the company paying your bills on the old house (while you're living in the new home) goes bankrupt? You join them in bankruptcy if you don't have the cash to pick up all the payments they fail to make! These are scams at high costs that should be avoided in ALL circumstances.

You also have to be careful with mortgage companies to make sure they are offering you the best rate. Some will offer you a rate much higher than you deserve in order to earn significantly more money on your mortgage origination. At times, these fees are hidden in the long-term APR. This business is full of sharks trying to take a bite out of your cash.

There is no easy way to buy and sell real estate. It's a complex transaction usually in the six or seven figures, where multiple industries converge in order for one transaction to close. In an age where many things that used to be complex have now become as easy as shouting "Alexa," real estate has seemingly gotten more difficult. Let's face it. I can shout "Alexa, order protein bars" then tomorrow they show up at my door. Why can't real estate simply be that easy?

Here's the truth: the convenience of shouting "Alexa" generally costs me a premium. Most everything I buy from Alexa/Amazon is 10 to 20% higher than shopping IN a Walmart. But, if I need $100 worth of items from Walmart, but Amazon will sell them to me by shouting at a speaker named Alexa for $112 and deliver them to my front door, why would I drive all the way to Walmart? My time and gas is worth $12.

Let's say I have a $100,000 home, and the market is hot. If I list the home with a top real estate agent at $100,000 and receive multiple offers in five days for a final sales price of $106,000, then I've taken the hard route (akin to driving to Wal-Mart).

Perhaps I should use Sam's Club as an example, because I can buy things substantially cheaper and in bulk there saving thousands of dollars per year in our household.

There are plenty of companies that want to convince me that real estate can be as easy is ordering from Alexa and Amazon. They have clever names like Knock.com, opendoor.com, Offerpad, 'guaranteed offer,' "if we can't sell it, we'll buy it" etc. These companies are the Amazon and Alexas of real estate. They offer what seems to be an easy transaction but at a premium cost.

Let's say I take the easy path and choose one of these companies mentioned above or the latest real estate agent promising to buy my home if he can't sell it, then what does it really cost me?

In the $100,000 home scenario the offer is typically more in line with $90,000. On top of that there's an 8 to 12% fee. The homeowner generally is convinced that all parties are in agreement on price and terms, until they conduct an inspection. That's where you get hit by the home sharks for another $5-10,000. In many cases, it's too late! You've already got a contract on another home (they've so conveniently helped you overpay for…).

Assuming you have no mortgage, you'd be lucky to receive a check at closing for $70-$78,000 for this $106,000 home. After paying a traditional real estate agent like me, you would have received a check for approximately $99,000. This means the premium for these "Alexa…order" services is 25 to 30% of your home's equity.

Because we live in a sharing economy where most household tasks have gotten far easier due to technology, we assume that can be the case for selling our home. It simply isn't.

Because of these misleading circumstances now populating the marketplace, combined with the consumer expectation of easier home sale transactions, the <u>unintelligent</u> homeowner falls for these scams and often has no choice but to move forward once they realize how much money they truly give away to these companies.

These housing sharks are further empowered by the sheer level of incompetence populating the housing industry as a whole. Being a listing agent and managing the showings of my sellers' homes is akin to running a kindergarten.

Notice I used kindergarten earlier in this book to describe dealing with the average real estate agent. This is not a joke: in fact, it's sad.

I have had hundreds of agents who simply don't have the basic intelligence to operate a pushbutton lockbox. I can't tell you the number of times I've had someone tell me a lockbox was broken only to drive to the house and find the box fully operational. The public school system in our country has clearly failed some in this industry!

Okay, that was a bit of a joke! But sadly, still true.

Housing is never going to be as easy as the rest of the technologically advanced economy. All of the financial industries that engage with the consumer are wrought with regulations by the federal government, and they see high levels of fraud combined with the lowest professional barrier to entry.

It takes roughly 1,000 hours to become a licensed massage therapist in most states. It takes just 60-75 hours to become licensed to handle the financial heartbeat of every household in our community: the home (the most expensive asset).

When you are buying or selling real estate and working with agents, hire a fighter who will admit how flawed and scandalous their industry is and will protect you from being bitten by the sharks.

This takes us to chapter 6: An industry full of frauds.

6 An industry full of frauds

We've covered a lot of ground on this topic already. In chapter 5, I discussed the "we buy your home" companies' main goal: make 20 to 30% off your home by helping you out of your equity.

Those companies are sort of benign compared to some that I've seen over the years.

I recently fired a property manager, who managed several properties of mine, for stealing my money. I had asked him several times to give me an accounting of a deposit of a tenant. These requests came in the form of multiple text messages and emails, along with a couple of phone calls over the course of a month. On the rare occasion I received an actual response, I was told "I'll look it up and get back to you tomorrow."

Tomorrow never came.

I fired this unresponsive property manager and scammer late on a Sunday evening. Within an hour, in an effort to save my business (I suppose), he finally sent me the information about the missing deposit. Aside from the fact that it was two months in the making (and thus illegal), it was also fraudulent. I accept that this could be simply the result of pure incompetence and not a calculated scam (but it's all the same to my bottom line whether intentional or accidental).

One of the line items that he had to pay out from my former tenant's deposit was the removal of all of her old furniture and trash (called a trash-out). There was a $300 charge for trash-out and a $200 charge for dumping.

I had been at the property a few weeks earlier with some workers I had renovating another townhome. I asked them to take a few minutes to help me remove all the furniture and trash from the property and they did. With my truck and trailer, I personally drove all the trash to the Union City, Georgia landfill and disposed of it.

You can imagine the embarrassment of the property manager when I produced the receipt showing that I had done the trash-out. Nonetheless, he tried to make it out as a mistake. It's always been odd to me that generally every mistake made by a real estate scammer is in their favor.

At the time of his firing, he was managing several of my properties. I had two new completions, the one with the previous eviction and a tenant to move out. Nearly five weeks had passed with this property manager not producing one tenant to sign a lease.

I had this property that I had been renovating and decided to put it on the market using First Multiple Listing Service (FMLS). Before doing that, I was talking to another owner who informed me that they were getting nearly $200 per month more for their units than mine which were almost identical. I decided to try what I thought was the top dollar for my rental and see what happened. Within 48 hours I had 50 phone calls and leased all the properties in the first week.

I'm telling you all this to illustrate incompetence and fraud at the same time. The government generally is policing the biggest fraud schemes. These are mortgage companies who harm thousands of clients to the tune of millions of dollars. These are real estate companies who steal millions of dollars in escrow deposits through Ponzi schemes. These scenarios are so common and so rampant in our marketplace, that the personal scenario I outlined above is not being policed at all. It's almost expected and common.

In reality, I was dealing with a property manager I am convinced was so greedy he was growing his business faster than he could keep up. In other words, he was incompetent. He had been effective, at a refreshing level, a couple years earlier when I hired him. When real estate businesses grow too fast, they actually start to make less money due to the resulting complexities and overhead. Most inexperienced brokers and managers fail to realize this until they learn it the hard way at your expense.

As a result they use situational ethics that significantly harm their clients. I believe this explains the attempt to steal the deposit that was ultimately due to me. Obviously, I ended up receiving the deposit. I was lucky, because most scenarios such as this result in an owner finding out that their property manager or real estate agent has already spent the money and doesn't have the capacity to repay it.

Based upon my vast experience in this industry, I would estimate that one out of two people holding a real estate license produces these kinds of circumstances for their clients. This means there is a 50% chance you will encounter someone who will steal your equity or throw it away due to their incompetence (or maybe both!).

I may be understating this problem by saying "50%."

It's easier to identify a competent crook than an incompetent fool. I have always said that an incompetent fool is more dangerous than a competent crook. A competent crook typically wants to steal your money and therefore they can be quickly identified and eliminated from your financial life (regardless of the damage).

By contrast, an incompetent fool tends to have the same impact on your financial life as the proverbial frog in the pot of warm water. The burners on the stove are on high. At first the frog feels very comfortable and cozy in the warm pot of water (p.s. you are the frog here). Before long, the frog is dead. He couldn't tell the difference between being warm and boiling because it happened so gradually..

If I didn't have experience in identifying these incompetent fools, this property manager would have cost me thousands of dollars, months of total vacancies, and thousands more in stolen profits over the next several months.

The reality is that I have seen so much fraud and illicit behavior in this industry that I simply don't trust anyone. Whether on my own behalf or on behalf of my clients, I frequently engage in what seems to be lengthy wasteful conversations with people I'm doing business with. The purpose of these conversations is to allow them to speak long enough that they start to show me who they really are.

I've always been told to allow people to tell you who they are and then believe them. Engaging in a lengthy professional conversation for no real reason is a great opportunity to see how often someone begins to contradict themselves.

In my last book, "The Trump in You," I joked about the fact that I've been known to conduct long listing presentations that can last two to three hours. Many people have commented over the years what a waste of time this seems to be or that I just like to hear myself talk.

In reality, I'm doing two things. I'm giving the potential home seller overwhelming evidence that I am consistent, that I care about them, and I won't waiver. I'm also interviewing them for as long as they'll have me to make sure that they are the same.

It is always in our mutual best interest to work with people we can trust. If a home-seller wishes for me to represent them in the sale of their $500,000 home where I'm likely to make a $15,000 commission, then the better our relationship, the more likely our success. If we have mutual respect and trust, then we will likely spend less time debating (re: distrusting) and more time strategizing on how to sell the home for the most money to the best buyer (re: person/buyer with an agent who will force them to overpay out of greed and desperation for commission).

The reality for home sellers is that the despicable nature of the real estate industry is our biggest threat and most important ally simultaneously. If we allow ourselves to be taken in by scam artists, we will be harmed. If you believe those risks and recognize the opportunity this presents, we will make more money. Here's what I mean: most real estate agents will subjugate even the simplest of their clients' interests for the smallest amount of money they can add to their bottom line. Remember, when the average agent does two or three deals per year, they have to make the most money possible on their two or three clients. They have a scarcity mentality. By contrast, I have an abundance mentality.

Since commissions are abundant, in my mind, being proud of my work becomes my point of focus. Finding reward (helping and teaching people to succeed) in your work can be hugely valuable.

Therefore, it is in my seller's best interest to find a buyer that has the most emotional attachment to the home and is willing to pay the most money. So, what is the secret to determining that?

There is no secret. With the vast majority of real estate agents, I simply pick up the phone, have a nice conversation with them, and ask. They will usually tell me everything I want to know, but shouldn't about their client.

Since I legally represent the seller in most transactions (and not the buyer), it makes complete sense that I then share that information (that the buyer's agent shouldn't have told me) with my seller. Such revelations, so easily obtained, can be worth thousands of dollars to the intelligent homeowners' bottom line.

It was long ago that I realized I can't change the illicit nature of the housing industry. I can write about it, talk about it, or even speak about it on the radio. I can even refuse to do business in such a dishonest and immoral way. However, I'm not going to stop it.

I frequently refer to myself as a "problem solver." I'd rather call myself that then say, Realtor. I've learned over the years that most everyone who puts the Realtor "R" on their car (or cards) is telling me that they're sheep in our industry. At some point, they were inducted as a Realtor and spent one day in orientation. Now they proudly display the "R" on their car. To me, this is a great way to say "I'm average."

When I discuss this on the radio, I frequently get hate mail. I'm not saying that every Realtor is average, illicit, or bad. What I am saying is that if you take all of the wonderful Realtors and combine them with those that are average and below average, you still have average.

Someone with the "Realtor-R" on their car, the "=" sign for fair housing, or a soccer ball (soccer mom agent which means part time) generally makes the worst representative for the intelligent homeowner. Those 'car symbols' represent sheep (go with the flow). I shouldn't have to advertise fair housing on my car. That is a minimum standard that I should never get close to. It's the law and it should be expected in EVERY transaction. Let me explain why these symbols are warning signs.

Our laws are not ethics or morals. They are a minimum set of rules that many people break every day. Ethics are generally situational. The average American, no matter how righteous, is generally situational with their ethics. Ethics are solely based upon interpretation because no one set of guidelines can apply to every scenario.

Morality on the other hand is about treating others exactly as you would want to be treated. Generally we want the best treatment, but sometimes giving the best treatment requires sacrifice. Morality is about integrity. This means that the best real estate agents aren't always the most likable because they're unwavering in their morality and integrity.

By contrast, compliant real estate agents are the kinds who believe that displaying logos on their vehicles makes them ethical, moral, or honorable. After all, I could put an Atlanta Falcons logo on my car instead of that equal sign. Why did I choose the "=" sign? Is it because I am promoting fair housing? Usually no! Most people put the "=" sign on the car for the same reason they put the Falcons logo on the car: to fit in with a specific crowd.

Here it is (the payoff to the soccer ball, the "=" sign, and the "R" logo): agents who first seek acceptance in their own industry are the ones most likely to favor the relationship with a broker or another agent over their own clients. In other words, if I want to appeal to my clients, I should probably put a dollar sign on my car next to the Realtor "R" with an "X" through it.

This all may sound silly, but it's true. You don't want sheep representing your highest financial interests. You want an individual who rises above the rest (better than average).

The soccer ball is simply a pet peeve of mine. My general rule of thumb is that if a real estate agent has a soccer ball on the back of their car, you are going to be in the backseat of that car in terms of their professional delivery of services. Those agents typically start their day late taking long lunches and end them early. While this becomes a bit comical when I tell the story on the radio, it's sadly true.

The best real estate agents would not put any logos or other industry paraphernalia on their vehicles. They either would leave their vehicles plain or specifically market themselves. People who display other businesses logos on their vehicle inherently don't understand individualism or marketing. In other words, self-promoters are usually the best at marketing for their clients too.

The people trying to tell you where they are associated and what they subscribe to in terms of ethics and equality are typically those practicing the least amount of it. In our history, they are typically the ones who decried people like me who constantly market my brand and craft as opposed to someone else's.

They have a hard time understanding marketing, their goal of getting you the most money for your home, or their fiduciary responsibility to serve your interests before those of their friends in the industry.

That statement brings me to another component of the real estate industry you need to be aware of for your own protection. Over the years, I've noticed a phenomenon of real estate agents seeming to worry more about how other real estate agents view them (as industry peers) than their clients. It's my contention that they believe they are only going to serve you one time (which in it of itself is small minded), instead of a lifetime, so they will negate your interests in favor of saving a relationship with another agent with whom they falsely believe may be more important to their career and future. The end result is less money for you and more money for them.

I've never really understood the reason for this stupidity. However, I believe it has something to do with being liked at the annual awards ceremony. I never attend those. I care what my clients think; not other agents. I've found my clients could care less about the awards I've received. They only care how fast and for how much money I will sell their house.

It is generally best to interview three professionals before hiring anyone in any industry. I generally like to pit those professionals against each other. I recently acquired the services of a major web vendor. I interviewed about five companies before choosing our current provider. I told each company which other four I was speaking with and asked them what they thought of their competitor.

I took note of the professionalism used to create differences between each other. By asking all five the same question I was able to develop repeated themes on certain companies. I quickly eliminated three companies, leaving only two competing. I then took them for a test run. I asked them to put me in touch with technical support for each company and I asked them for specific and challenging resolutions to my individual concerns.

One company blew the other company out of the water with their ability to create workarounds for unique requests that I would have as a client.

Let me translate this to real estate. I recently had a client who said they wanted their agent to be present for every showing. In the scammer world of real estate I'm describing here, most agents would simply say "absolutely, I will be at every showing no problem." That's a lie!

No productive real estate agent needs to be present for every showing. If a real estate agent is making that as an honest commitment, they just don't have much business and thus don't have the experience to give you the best results.

I was honest with the seller. I said, "I am a very busy agent and there is no way that I can commit to being present at every showing, even if I was your next-door neighbor." I offered an alternative solution.

Without going into their personal details, there was a specific room in the house that was a concern because of its contents. Fortunately, it was a secondary bedroom. I suggested that we take a couple of photos of that room, frame them, and post them on the door leaving it locked for showings. I also suggested putting a security camera which could be enabled for showings and disabled while the seller was home. I further suggested that if someone needed to see that room during the second showing, I would personally drive to the home, unlock it, and be responsible for securing it when done.

Instead of telling the seller what they wanted to hear, I told them the truth. Notwithstanding these solutions that I offered, it is very disturbing to homebuyers to have the seller or their representatives in the home during a showing. It's one of the worst marketing ideas peddled in the real estate industry.

Put yourself in a buyer's shoes. If you are viewing a home that you are thinking about buying, you want to be in the home alone without feeling any pressure, so you can get comfortable with its environment. Having a seller or their agents spying on you tends to disrupt that necessary process.

After outlining this fact to the seller, I specifically addressed their concerns and offered them a fail proof solution to managing their security issues.

In an earlier chapter, I described that many times the best sales professionals will challenge your way of thinking or even debate you. I did that here. It would have been far easier to simply tell the seller exactly what they wanted to hear, albeit a lie. That's what this industry does.

The most successful real estate agents don't. There are very few of us in the industry.

I could write a whole book about the scams that I've endured or fought against for my clients. The bottom line is that if you're in Georgia, and you hire my team, you don't have to be on the lookout for scams; that's my job.

If you're anywhere else in the country, I could say good luck. But I'll give you a better option. If you allow me to refer you to the agent in your marketplace that I trust the most, then I will be one phone call away anytime you buy and sell real estate with them to make certain that whatever you're facing is not a scam.

I'll make one additional commitment to you: unlike much of my industry, I'll admit if I'm not qualified to answer a question in your housing marketplace. In such a case, I will help you find someone that is.

If this sounds like a sales pitch, or you don't trust it, that's fine. But, please find someone that you can trust to be your real estate guide wherever you do business in the future.

Unless you are selling homes for clients to the tune of dozens per year, you cannot possibly protect yourself well enough because you will not have the experience with the latest scams and tricks that are designed to steal your equity.

All that said, now we get to the most valuable chapter of this book. I'm going to tell you how to find the best deals in housing. In fact, this chapter is so invaluable that it almost instructs you not to use the real estate buyers' agent in the process.

That's next.

7 FINDING THE BEST DEALS

If you've sold several homes over the years, you may not need a real estate agent to do what's in this chapter. It would be a good idea, but it's not entirely necessary. By contrast, if this is your first, second, or third home purchase (whether as an investment or primary residence), you would be insane not to hire a real estate agent to help you do that.

You'll need to read this whole chapter to understand the parameters of what I've described above. Especially for my radio career, I've received hundreds of phone calls from people who wish to 'get into' real estate investing. Almost all of them, no matter how long they have listened to me, seemed to have not listened at all. They are on the road at 100 miles an hour in the wrong direction.

I generally don't like working with investors. Don't get me wrong. If I'm working with the right kind of investors, it's fun, rewarding, and easy. But most investors have no idea what they're doing.

During the financial crash from 2009 to 2013 I worked with hundreds of investors who purchased from one of the many scam artists (re: agents) I discussed in the last chapter. Their previous real estate agent sold them on speculation, diminished the necessity of cash flow, and convinced them to buy properties that ultimately ended up in foreclosure ruining their financial lives. My job was to rescue them. 99% of the time that's exactly what I did.

What I saw were a bunch of people who had the right idea about investing in real estate. They simply ran into the wrong real estate agent. The real estate agent encouraged them to use their emotions to buy the homes as opposed to analytics. Real estate investing is strictly about cash flow and it should almost never be about speculation unless you're already independently wealthy and can lose money on a property for a short period of time because of its likelihood to appreciate quickly. This almost never works except for the most experienced and sophisticated real estate investors.

The best investors for my business are those who rarely use me to buy a home but almost always use me to sell a home. These are people who call me with the property they are about to purchase from a direct seller, without real estate agent involvement, and simply want my opinion. I've often been willing to dispense this opinion, with an agreement that once they are ready to sell that property they will list it with me.

It may not surprise you how few people actually take me up on this offering. They would rather do it themselves than admit they don't know enough about doing it. Additionally, many of them are afraid to commit to paying me a 6% commission for helping them make an extra 10 to 20% out of fear they'll miss the opportunity to find someone that might do it for substantially lower commission. In the end, they end up with a real estate scam artist who costs far more than 6% while they make virtually nothing (while taking all the risk).

The purpose of this chapter is not to continue the last chapter about scam artists in the business. I simply wanted to set the stage before I tell you all the secrets to buying the right properties. Remember, I told you that you make your money when you buy not when you sell. Therefore, my willingness to advise people who might buy a property where I don't receive a commission is an added value (that I offer) since I make my money from the part of the process where you lose the most. I want to make sure you earn the most money on each deal since I'm involved in the most expensive part of the process.

Because I've bought and sold hundreds of properties and represented thousands, I can sometimes accomplish in a few minutes what some investors could spend a week attempting to determine. Over time, these investors will develop that same skill. Unfortunately, most of them allow their ego to block their ability to receive this helpful instruction and risk mitigation.

Now, the part you've been waiting for.

How do you find the best deals?

The best deals exist where you have the least competition. As a buyer you want to be the only buyer interested in that property at that time. This means turning to real estate agents on the multiple listing service is unlikely to produce that result unless the market is in calamity. The best properties for investors are properties that are not listed in conventional ways. Here's the list:

- Probate. At times the family simply wants to sell the property because it's too emotionally troublesome to deal with it. In some ways, buying via discount is a bigger help to them than you can imagine. It gets it over with for them and gives you a great price.
- One of my favorite ways to buy property is 'the grass test.' If the grass is two feet high or more, there's an opportunity there. If your real estate agent (re: someone like me who helps you on the way in so I get the listing on your way out) becomes your partner, they'll probably give you the name,

mailing address, emails, and phone number of the owner. The technology we already have at our fingertips is incredible.
- Divorce sales. In most cases, the home needs to be sold quickly in a divorce. These are all public records.
- Bankruptcies. At times, the chapter 7 bankruptcy trustee keeps a list of properties that need to be sold quickly. Call them. Sometimes they have an agent. You can also lookup bankruptcy cases on federal court websites and see if there are properties associated with the filing. Contact the owner and make an offer. The trustee will have to approve it.
- Short sales. Because you can be tied up for a long time waiting on short sale approvals, most homebuyers don't want to risk losing other homes while waiting on these. This leaves investors the most likely candidates to purchase short sales, which are homes where the seller owes more than it's worth.
- Foreclosures. Buying homes on the courthouse steps can sometimes be an incredible opportunity. Banks make mistakes with these because they have so many of them across the country. We recently saw a bank sell a $400,000 home for $146,000 on the courthouse steps. Here's a hint: all the real estate sheep show up in the most popular counties. When I lived in Charleston, the Charleston County courthouse steps were always overflowing. It's the same in Fulton County in Atlanta, Georgia. Go to the counties where there are the fewest people and you'll find the best deals with the least bidding competition.
- REO companies. These companies help banks dispose of their properties that were taken back in foreclosure. They usually display their future listings well before they hit the MLS. If possible, doing cursory inspections on a few properties before they hit the multiple listing service. This can give you the advantage of making an offer the moment it

becomes available and removing all contingencies, thus making your offer the most attractive of all. Banks hate contingencies in contracts.

- Be able to make cash offers whenever possible. Remember a cash offer is any offer that involves the seller receiving cash at closing. Even if you finance 150% of the purchase price with a traditional bank, that is still a cash offer. If you have the cash to purchase without a mortgage, and are willing to risk doing so, then make a no financing contingency offer which is far more valuable. Just know, that if you get declined for financing you will have to part with your cash in order to make the purchase. You'll win far more deals at far better prices if you can remove the financing contingency legitimately without putting yourself in financial risk. Cash at closing is the only way real estate is purchased. Deciding to use a mortgage, so long as you close on time is not a violation of the contract. You simply have to be able to perform if that mortgage falls apart for you.

- Word-of-mouth. Everyone knows someone who owns a home and is going through a rough time. In many cases, the distressed homeowner is so distraught over their entire financial circumstance, they do not have the emotional capacity to even think about dealing with their home. Many people believe that investors showing up with a lowball offer is shady. In some cases, it may be. In others, you may just save that homeowner from procrastinating with their home sale problem and losing all of their equity in foreclosure. I think everyone would agree that helping someone facing foreclosure quickly make some money now instead of nothing in foreclosure is a win-win circumstance.

- Advertising. "We buy houses" advertising works. There's nothing more I have to say about that. In fact, I do it. And if I have a list of serious investors who will purchase properties I identify for a reasonable fee, I'll do it for you. Advertising that you buy houses is simply a great way to reach people desperate to sell in any market condition.

- Tax sales. These are very complex and I don't recommend it, without further education. That said, buying a property for $40,000 that's worth $250,000 is a no-brainer. Just understand that regardless of what anyone tells you, you need a few hundred thousand dollars to deploy into tax sale certificates in order to even have the hope that a homeowner doesn't redeem their delinquent taxes and take the property back. If they do, you'll make a handsome return on your money (sometimes up to 12%), but the endgame is to invest in the real estate. This process is best for people with a seven-figure net worth (although not limited to those with six-figures). If your net worth is under $250,000 this is not the place I recommend you start.
- Government seizure and forfeiture. Purchasing these properties is a complex scenario and requires more reading. However, if you follow this process and understand purchasing criteria, you can find incredible properties that the government has seized as a result of criminal activity and needs to dispose of in order to repay the victims. You can not only serve a great cultural and civic purpose here, you can also make great money.
- Struggling businesses. Struggling business owners, nearing bankruptcy or already in it, frequently have properties that can be sold at substantial discounts generating lifesaving capital for the business.
- Rough parts of town. Most investors converge on the hottest, latest area with redevelopment. By the time that's obvious, it's too late. The best investments for this kind of living are those

where you can buy before redevelopment comes into the community and hold them for substantial returns via rental income while you wait.
- Buy a whole street. This is for the more advanced investor, but if you can buy several homes for $20,000-30,000 each on the same street you can literally rehab a neighborhood. There is a large amount of money to be made doing this, but you need plenty of capital because contractors are frequently worse than real estate agents (so you'll need a good one).

These are the basic elements I've used over my two decades of real estate investing to make millions of dollars in profits. I've advised hundreds of potential investors on these opportunities only to realize that they find it too complex and too much work. Regretfully, there are a number of systems (re: scams) being peddled in our industry that give the impression that making $30,000 on a home flip is easy. The reality is that in order to buy one property I typically have to review about 100. Notice I say "review." Showings are a waste of time unless you plan to buy the property.

By the time you reach my acumen level, you rarely visit these properties. If a visit is necessary, in order for the property to make a short list, then I usually have a runner or assistant take dozens of photographs. I have even bought property sight unseen by having a paid professional do a virtual tour via FaceTime or Skype of the property. Buying 15 or 20 homes a year as I've done on occasion, I literally have to sort through 2000 homes in order to isolate those opportunities. For me, it's very analytical.

For the average buyer turn investor, it's imperative for you to see hundreds of homes during the process of buying your first two or three. Unfortunately, most investors apply their own personal needs and wants in homeownership to their investments.

I live in Buckhead, a very nice area in North Atlanta. I rarely see anything that is remotely attractive as an investment in this area. By contrast, many people who live in Buckhead love the community so much (as do I), they are emotionally attached to it and feel that it is a good investment. That is a perfect way to lose money. I have never understood the people who invest in a $400,000 condo in order to rent it for $3000 a month. There are areas of Metro Atlanta where I can spend $150,000 on three properties and earn the same $3000 per month. In terms of cash return, I can make two or three times the money in less desirable areas than those that are most desirable.

The best investments are those that need significant or substantial rehabilitation. There is less financing available for those properties and fewer people willing to take what is the perceived risk of repairing them. For property investors, damage and repairs are opportunity as much as they are liability.

Here's a hint: If you are buying a $100,000 property that needs $20,000 in repairs, for $60,000, you'll be fine. Stop worrying! You SHOULD NOT buy a $100,000 property that needs $20,000 in repairs for $80,000. If a seller wants me to buy their 'dump' wrought with deferred maintenance than I expect a discount of 100% of the costs required to get it back to average market condition. This means $20,000 in repairs should net you a $40,000 discount off repaired market value. After all, you're the one who has to hassle with contractors, repairs and risk!

Buying properties that have been well maintained or rehabbed generally cost more than those that are uninhabitable and need a lot of work. A lot of the profit that these get-rich-quick people describe is best described as sweat equity. Somehow, they don't bother to tell you that before they collect the $5000 they charge for their seminars.

8 THE PHILOSOPHY OF HOME PRICING

Here's something that very few people in the real estate industry will ever admit: we don't know how to price homes. Let me qualify that statement.

Perhaps a better way to put it would be that only arrogant people try to convince you that they're an expert in pricing homes. Appraisers don't know how to price homes. They know how to tell you what the value **was**. Real estate agents generally don't know how to price homes because they have no training whatsoever in doing so. Their approach to home pricing is what they feel. Unintelligent homeowners, which are most home sellers on the market today, don't know how to price homes. They simply want more than their home is worth. After all, who doesn't?

So how the heck do you price your home to make sure that you get the most money for it? The answer lies in price trending.

When the market was collapsing in 2008-2011, price-trending was imperative for the real estate agents that were still making money. If a $100,000 home was declining in price by $1500 per month during the height of the housing collapse, and such depreciation had been occurring for the last several months, pricing was easy. Every month, the home was losing 1.5% of its value. If two identical homes sold last month for $100,000, then the same home would be worth $98,500 this month. In a market where there were 10,000 homes for 300 buyers, pricing and market value still wasn't enough.

The only way to sell the home was at a discount. If I hired an appraiser to price that same $100,000 home, he or she would've looked at the past six months and perhaps told me the home was worth $105,000. If I asked the typical so-called real estate professional they would either tell me what I want to hear ($105-110,000) or, at best, $100,000. Some would be lying and some simply uninformed.

For the sellers who actually needed to sell the home immediately, solutions were lacking. I used price trending. Since homes were depreciating at 1.5% per month based on the previous value of $100,000 as of a month ago, I had my work cut out for me. The seller's home was already worth $98,500 (less than anything identical to them). And, if I didn't sell it in the first 30 days it would be worth significantly less months from now.

Three months of trending has always worked well for me. Since the market was declining at 1.5% per month, the three-month price was $94-$95,000. Under the same trend, the same home would be worth in the low $80,000s a year from now. My job was to get the former and avoid the latter. I had the uphill battle of convincing my sellers, one by one, to sell for below market value now as opposed to substantial losses later.

When the crisis first erupted, dozens of my home sellers had equity in their homes but had fallen behind on their mortgage payments. We got them checks (paid to them) at closing for equity that would have evaporated months later. By selling slightly below market, because pricing was trending significantly downward, we actually saved the sellers tens of thousands of dollars in future equity loss in the process.

Fast forward a decade and we're doing the exact opposite. Identical homes selling for $100,000 last month (if that even exists now at $100k), while experiencing an appreciation rate of 1.5%, are now worth far more than any real estate agent or appraisal will suggest. This means the appraisal price is dangerous and yet again the real estate community is wholly uninformed on how to price a home.

In this reverse, hot market scenario, if prices are rising at 1.5% per month on this $100,000 home, why can we not do the exact opposite of what we did in 2008 to 2011? We can.

Believe me when I say it's far more enjoyable to convince a seller to overprice their home than it is to underprice it!

If the home is now worth $101,500 (which means Zillow's Zestimate is probably $94,000 - way too low), it will be worth close to $105,000 in three months.

Since most real estate agents only sell two or three homes per year they couldn't possibly have any experience with a similar home in the recent few months. After all, they don't sell much! Since we recently had several homes in various price categories, relevant to this scenario, we know that multiple offers are coming in within days at higher than list price, which is already higher than the recent sales. This house should be priced, depending on its condition, between $109,900 and $114,500.

My guess is that it will sell at near full price if not over it and that the appraisal will come in slightly below our sales price. That's as of 2018 based upon what we're experiencing under $500,000 in Metro Atlanta. Obviously the circumstances and conditions change constantly.

There are very few homes for sale at $100,000 anymore. I use that price because it's easy to illustrate the math. In reality, we're seeing the scenario in much higher prices as well.

Price trending is a way to maximize the equity from your home without attempting to time the market for its highest point. Most of the homes selling in markets where prices are appreciating are selling so quickly because they are underpriced due to the incompetence of the agents used by unintelligent homeowners.

The intelligent homeowner chooses an agent who knows how to price trend the market so that if it's falling in price they do not lose any more equity. However, if the market is appreciating in price they grab some of the future equity by tapping into the resulting feeding frenzy that is driving prices up.

In normal market scenarios where there is limited appreciation (4-5%), price trending still applies but with a much more moderate application. If there is no appreciation, then pricing is easy because you simply put the price in line with the last few home sales that offer equal location, size, and features.

9 EMOTION WILL COST YOU

This chapter will serve as a 'canary in the coal mine' for most intelligent homeowners. The most difficult challenge I have faced in my real estate career is attempting to get certain clients out of their own way.

In my earlier years I found myself caring more for the client than they cared for themselves. As I became more experienced, I learned to match their level of care if at all possible. You can go crazy quickly in the real estate business if you care more for the people that hire you than they do for themselves.

The big challenge I face with homeowners is their emotions. I'm reminded of a specific seller I had a couple of years ago. They had a very clean home, and they had already bought their next one, so the home we were selling was vacant. As a result, it had a 'cold' feeling and looked a little bit dated. Under every imaginable circumstance, if I had owned that home, I would've staged it.

Prices were rising in the immediate marketplace and there was significant demand around that price point. We had 21 showings in the first 19 days the home was on the market. Almost every point of feedback commented that the home's condition or price was the problem.

As I did in the last chapter, I used price trending to recommend the list price of the home. On paper, it was worth approximately $250,000. We listed it for $269,900 (These aren't the real numbers - however, they are the same percentages. The real numbers were even higher).

I received an email after the first 20 days from one of the two sellers complaining about the lack of activity on the property. I almost fell out of my chair. Thinking that I had gone crazy over night, I went back through each of the feedback forms I had forwarded to both of my sellers. After realizing that I had not gone crazy, I replied back to the seller that averaging nearly a showing per day, consistently, for almost three weeks is well above any expectations that any of us should've had. I reiterated that staging the home was the problem.

I told the seller that if they were unwilling to stage the home that our pricing strategy need to be adjusted. One of the things that homeowners don't understand is that when someone says that the pricing is a problem, that's not always true.

Remember, we've already established that real estate agents have no idea how to price a home. Therefore, having one of them give us feedback this is a home is priced too high is not always useful. I only find that feedback valuable if it's an agent that I recognize and whose opinion I respect. Comments on pricing by rather inexperienced, typical agents usually mean that the homes they are seeing at that price point are in better condition than this one. So, how do we fix that?

We stage the home so that it looks like a home in much better condition than it really is. I'm not suggesting that we cover-up flaws. Rather, I'm suggesting that we stage it so that it has a warmer and more welcoming feeling that it presently does.

Over the next few weeks I attempted to explain this phenomenon to the seller ad nauseam. The seller couldn't get out of her own way.

Her solution was for me to conduct a broker's open house and a regular open house. After all, since the home wasn't selling, I must have had no idea what I was talking about and since she knew everything, I needed to be punished. Therefore if I would spend an entire day parading agents who sell two homes per year through the home, along with neighbors who might become our competition and sell their own home, that would make her feel better.

It would make more sense putting HGTV-like furniture in the home and taking new photos that would make it so much more appealing they could sell in a matter of days. I refused to do the open houses because it simply was not part of my marketing plan and was never discussed.

I brought up staging at the initial listing presentation before they ever agreed to list the home with me. They told me they would consider staging if the home wasn't sold in the first two to four weeks. It had now been two months. I became convinced that one of the sellers was more worried about proving me wrong than actually selling the home. It was at this point that I addressed the situation with the husband privately.

As a result, he became my only point of contact in the transaction. We talked through a number of strategies and executed some of the recommendations I'd been making (although limited in terms of staging), and successfully sold the home in two weeks. It sold for $15,000 more than the expectations I had set based upon our price trending analysis.

I'm always cautious with setting expectations. My goal is to always exceed the expectations I set and not go below them. I set the expectations of a low $250s sales price for recommending a list price near $270. We sold it in the mid-$260s. I believe we would've sold it for full price in the first week had the seller taken my staging advice.

The cost of staging would've been $1750 paid by the seller. I've done it dozens of times on my own properties and rarely have one on the market for more than two or three weeks in any market. Because the seller was unwilling to spend the $1750, I believe they sold it two months late for $4000 less than they would've gotten the first week.

This means emotions, arrogance, and pride of one of the sellers cost them two months of market time ($2000/month mortgage) and $4000 (minus staging costs saved) in sales price. Net costs for the emotional seller?

$5250.

What's sad is that this seller had no idea that they couldn't get out of their own way. I netted a commission and a bad review for this transaction.

The lesson I learned is one that should be mutually applicable to both real estate agents and intelligent homeowners: when someone is not functionally aspiring to the goal at hand, they should be fired. If I promise the seller things that I don't do, they should fire me. That was not the case here. Rather, they induced me into the listing by leading me to believe they would stage the home. Once they began asking me to do things that were not part of our initial discussions, and that I have specific evidence of not working, I should've parted ways.

My goal is to turn every home seller client into a positive review and advocate referring me business in the future. No single commission is worth a home seller leaving a bad review and spreading negativity about my honest hard work and efforts (especially when they are the problem).

Too frequently, emotions cloud our best decisions. In many cases, I can't desire for my client to have a better experience than they will create for themselves. I can only serve them to the level for which they will allow me to serve.

In a general sense, emotional decision-making is the number one reason that real estate markets boom and bust and rarely operate in between. People convince themselves that prices are going up by their own intelligence and acumen. For the sake of feeling good, they convince themselves that prices will never fall again.

When they lose substantially, they convince themselves that they had nothing to do with the market and that it will never return again. Misery loves company and it's easy to blame what is or isn't happening on everything but ourselves.

As a result, most unintelligent homeowners continue to make the wrong decisions in the wake of a series of wrong decisions already made. Generally, candid and straightforward agents like me endure the most punishment for attempting to save them from themselves.

The intelligent real estate agent, which I've become, understands that once we attempt to help someone get out of their own way, and they lash out at us for doing so, we either have to end the relationship or work within a narrow path of attempting to serve their best interests but not providing them with the best advice (for fear of constant backlash). The best results are usually commensurate with more work.

The intelligent homeowner never creates a scenario where financial experts of any kind ever fear or regret being candid with them because of their emotional reactions.

Once you isolate yourself on an island away from candor and accountability, failure becomes inevitable at multiple levels.

You shouldn't fall in love with the house at any point during the search, purchase, or ownership process. It will guide you to make decisions that will harm your financial interests and create malignancy in other areas of your life.

When selling a home, you shouldn't allow the behavior of the homebuyer or candor of real estate agent to cloud the number one goal you set forth to accomplish: obtaining the highest net sales price for the home.

Nothing else matters when you're selling a home except net sales price. Too many sellers get caught up in the emotions of what I call the "I didn't haves." Closing costs paid by a seller on behalf of a buyer is a recurring theme of "I didn't haves." "No one paid my closing costs when I bought it, so I'm not paying for your closing costs." I've always found this scenario troubling. Who cares if you pay someone's closing costs so long as you hit your bottom line?

If I set out to net $200,000 on the home and the buyer is offering $210,000 and asking me to pay $5000 of their closing costs, why do I care? If I am meeting or exceeding my goal that is all that should matter.

Unfortunately, too many unintelligent homeowners allow what they feel to instruct how they act.

The market does not care what you feel the home is worth. The market does not care about your personal upgrades. The market does not care how your family felt living in the home. The market does not care how well you cared for the home. These may be harsh statements to tolerate especially in homes that have been over improved or upgraded beyond what the market requires or maintained beyond average.

Homeowners who have been meticulous, emotional, and careful with their homes as an extension of their own pride, frequently cost themselves more money attempting to recoup their efforts or investments that exceed expected averages.

As an intelligent homeowner, you should always be calculating the improvements in sweat equity you invest in your home to make certain that you get the full enjoyment out of it while expecting very little return if any from those things.

To do otherwise will cost you dramatically.

10 PRIVATE MONEY LOANS

The biggest challenge to real estate wealth building is capital. Finding money to acquire real estate, make necessary repairs, and manage cash flow is a daunting task especially for new investors.

The reality is that there is plenty of money available. Most people just don't want to pay the price for it. By the time you apply for conventional investor mortgage in order to purchase a property that you intend to rehab and flip quickly, you have likely spent more time qualifying for the mortgage, through some idiotic underwriter, than the time you will invest in the property rehab. This is no understatement!

I believe the best way to own investment grade rental real estate of any kind is with no mortgage. Even then, obtaining a mortgage on a primary residence (let alone an investment) becomes extremely painful. Even though you own properties with no debt, conventional underwriters still underwrite each of your properties as though they do.

If you own several properties with or without a mortgage, the amount of paperwork required to underwrite just one purchase or refinance can be hundreds of pages. A normal loan can take 20 to 30 days. As you begin to own a few investment properties, closing a new loan, with a typical underwriter, can take weeks.

The best deals do not afford you the opportunity to spend weeks in underwriting. Aside from that reality, we only have so much time. I find that my time is far more valuable than a few percentage points of interest and weeks of arguing with an idiotic underwriter.

The standard mortgage underwriting process is for sheep. These are people with great credit scores, one job, barely any savings and no real investments other than their 401(k) or IRA. In other words, banks prefer to lend money to people with great credit who plan to work until they're dead. If you get some wild idea that you want to create real wealth through real estate investment and own several properties, good luck in the conventional mortgage process. Banks don't like people who have financial independence and security.

Having said all that, it may still come as a surprise that I am perfectly willing to pay 8 to 10% interest to avoid this nightmare. I prefer crowd-sourced lending or private moneylending.

Private moneylending is always the cheapest because it usually involves borrowing money from someone who has a lot of cash but no idea what to do with it. Offering them one or two points of origination (a percentage of the total loan) and 8 to 10% interest is a wonderful opportunity for them. For you, it saves you an incredible amount of time and costs associated with the standard loan.

Let's say you're thinking about borrowing money at 5% from 'First National Bank of Hell.' It's an appropriate name, because that's about what the experience will be: hell. Let's say the loan is $100,000. In a typical scenario closing costs will be about $3500 at closing. If you plan to keep the property roughly nine months (hopefully far less), then you'll pay another $3750 in interest during that time.

Let's further assume that my final sales value on the property is $160,000 and my total investment not counting closing costs and interest is $110,000. After commissions on the resale (along with closing costs), I will net $147,200. After deducting $7250 in loan origination costs and interest, my net is just under $30,000.

This all sounds great, right? Wrong!

Most of the properties that present these sorts of opportunities need to close in three to four weeks from contract ratification. The lending scenario I described above for the average investor is a two or three month underwriting process. Even assuming that I can convince a seller to wait through this process, which is highly unlikely, in the amount of time spent dealing with the 'First National Bank of Hell,' I literally could have acquired another rehab using a much easier private or crowd-sourced lending scenario.

In that scenario, I would have probably paid $6500 in points and fees at closing and $6750 in interest over those nine months (assuming an average 9% rate). Instead of earning roughly $30,000 on that first scenario, my net would have been roughly $25,000.

Instead of spending weeks arguing with an idiotic underwriter at the 'First National Bank of Hell,' I could've spent that time much more pleasurably acquiring and rehabbing a second property. With virtually the same amount of effort and similar risk I've now earned about $49,000 in income instead of $30,000. In reality, that cheap money from 'First National Bank of Hell' actually cost me $19,000 in additional profit due to wasted time.

The reality of these scenarios is that you always want money the cheapest you can get it and with the fewest hassles. As an investor, it's always better to have sources of guaranteed money that are easy to acquire and rapid to close. If you have great credit, there are scenarios where refinancing out of a high interest private money loan into a conventional underwritten loan make sense.

However, attempting to buy properties that afford you the opportunity to make tens of thousands of dollars in profit while obtaining the lowest rates available on the market is nearly impossible. After all, the main reason you're getting such a discount and opportunity in the first place is because of your ability to close in a week or two. That's simply not going to happen unless you have cash from an equity line of credit already established.

Obviously, if you have substantial equity in a property and can qualify for an equity line of credit, that is the ideal way to purchase and flip investment property. Home equity line of credit (HELOC) money is typically one of the lowest cost financing on the market and it allows you to write a check at closing when you purchase a property and repay the loan immediately when you sell it. In this scenario no bank controls the property you are purchasing or selling since the HELOC is attached to another property you are not planning to sell.

My company outsources to a couple of the top private money lending institutions in the country. Go to therealestateexperts.com to learn more ("financing" tab, then "private money"). If you cannot establish a HELOC and don't have a relative or colleague to offer you a cheaper private money alternative (which I would always recommend over my option), then our private money sourcing is one of the fastest and most reliable on the market today, as of this writing.

11 NEGOTIATION

I was first published nationally in 2005 in a book called "The Advantage of Real Estate." I wrote a single chapter in that book about negotiation.

Since that time our culture and business dynamics have changed dramatically. Facebook, Twitter, and Instagram have become almost as commonplace in our lives as a cell phone was then. Our cell phones have become our computers and our music players.

In 2005, negotiation was typically done via limited means via telephone or via email. That is no longer the case nor recommendable. The options for negotiation now include Facebook, texting, telephone, email, and a host of other digital options. These options can be overwhelming and confusing and make it incredibly difficult to determine how to proceed as an intelligent homeowner attempting to sell or buy a piece of real estate.

In my negotiations, one thing has never changed. I've always sought to know the most possible about the people I'm negotiating against. Now, their entire life story is available at my disposal.

The reality is that all this technology has created a propensity for people to present a fake version of themselves at every step of their lives. As a culture, we spend a great deal of time enhancing our image on social media. We project a false image of what's really happening in our lives in an attempt to be viewed as someone to be envied because of how great our world is. The gravity of this false image we project is different from each person to the other.

The fact remains that over time, unwittingly, we tell the truth about who we really are.

However, I find that most people are operating in a zone between totally disingenuous and outright lying, especially when dealing with real estate.

Most buyers will pay more than the articulated top dollar. Most sellers will take less than their articulated bottom dollar. I've never found this to be anything but factual. People never tell what they will actually do: instead, they tell you what they want.

Assuming this reality in every situation is already a huge game changer for you when negotiating a real estate deal. Even as your advocate, agent, or friend, I've learned to assume that what you tell me you will do or not do is not always the case. Why would you assume any differently about those you negotiate against in a transaction?

The next negotiation tactic is to watch for inconsistencies in statements. I recently had an agent bring me a contract on one of my listings and he told me that this buyer was fully underwritten with the mortgage company. As a real estate listing agent, whose fiduciary responsibility is to represent the best interest of my clients, such a statement is like 'gold to my ears.' However, since we've already established that I don't trust anyone or anything, I asked for a copy of the approval letter.

The letter was a standard pre-approval letter that stated they had pulled the borrowers credit and had reviewed their income information. It said nothing about having the loan fully underwritten and approved as was indicated to me. As a result, we asked for an updated statement from their mortgage company reflecting the actual reality of their present approval status.

What we received was that the automated underwriting system had approved them, and the underwriter had verified their income statements as matching their stated income. We also found out in the scenario that they were a self-employed borrower. Knowing that an underwriter had their income statements and stated that she would accept them as-is was very helpful.

As a result of this negotiation, we raised the requirement of earnest money and shortened some of their contingency periods.

By this point it won't be shocking for you to hear the number of times I have been told one thing and found the reality to be completely different. The first rule of negotiation is to assume that whatever you're being told can only be accepted when it's in writing. Even then, I have found 'reasonable evidence' to have been fabricated.

If reasonable evidence is fabricated in order to induce us into a decision or contract ratification, we at least have the essence of bad faith and default, as leverage on our side, in the event the deal unravels. I am always looking for ways to keep the leverage on my or my client's side.

I could write an entire book about how to keep the leverage on our side of the transaction. Most people hire me because of my vast amount of skill and ability in negotiations. The best way to learn how to negotiate contracts is to simply negotiate dozens of them. A smart person never makes the same mistake twice.

The foregoing paragraph probably doesn't give you much comfort if you're buying a home in Minnesota. However, I offered to solve that problem for you earlier if you'll allow me to refer you to an agent you can use in that marketplace. This means two things for you: First, I will use my experience to identify a qualified agent in ways that you may not be able to. Second, I will be just one phone call away if anything starts to look suspicious. Having a license in a particular state is not necessary to dispense direct advice. I can generally tell if something is right or wrong and help you identify another professional to help you avoid getting trapped in a mess.

An intelligent homeowner selling a house typically does all the wrong things. In their defense, this is usually out of a willingness to be as transparent as possible and morally upstanding. Most of the clients I attract are honorable people who simply want to do the right thing while getting the most money for their home.

Regretfully, the real estate culture does not always reward 'doing the right thing.'

I'm reminded of a seller who came to me during the height of the financial crash. He made good money and had a home worth approximately $1 million. His first mortgage was close to $1 million and a second mortgage was close to $500,000. For months, he had been making his payments and attempting to negotiate with the 'First National Bank of Hell.' If I'm not careful, you might figure out who this bank really is.

He had offered to sell his home, pay off the first mortgage, and make annual payments on the remaining $500,000 for the next few years until it was paid in full. In other words, he had agreed to take the full financial hit on this property in order to stop the nightmare of monthly payments and the continued decline in value. 'The First National Bank of Hell' basically told him to 'pack sand.' They were unwilling to help even though he was absolutely doing the right thing.

With property values continuing to decline, doing the right thing meant selling the property as quickly as possible before it lost more value, leaving him and the bank in a much worse financial predicament.

Like hundreds of others sellers, he had heard me on the radio talking about these things and called me. We met in my office, I referred him to a top lawyer with a great deal of experience in these situations, and we embarked upon a short sale process. He was advised legally by the lawyer to stop making his payments if he wanted any hope of resolving the situation.

Within a few months, the bank approved a short sale releasing him from all of his deficient liability. Due to the legalities of this particular situation and federal government oversight, the bank also had to pay him a settlement as part of this transaction.

Here was a guy willing to do the right thing and instead our collective industries made that impossible. He couldn't hold onto the property any longer because the payments were killing him and the value was plummeting. That would not have been the right thing either. But, he couldn't bring half a million dollars to closing which meant he was stuck.

In real estate, when you see a light at the end of the tunnel, assume it's an oncoming train. If you stay on the tracks, you're going to get 'run over.' While he was presently paying his mortgage, there was no surety that he would be able to continue paying the mortgage into the future. My justification for the decisions he made was simple.

The property value was continuing to decline. The bank would not assist him in mitigating their mutual damages at his sole expense. Therefore, he had no choice but to mitigate his own and then to negotiate with the bank on the deficiency balance. Because of the stupidity of the 'First National Bank of Hell,' they offered to release him in full, and he accepted.

Had they done the right thing when he first approached them to help the bank and the customer mitigate their damages, they would've lost no money.

As a contrast to that situation, I have encountered a number of people who were manipulating the bank, under the same conditions, by fighting foreclosure so that they can keep their properties as rentals and earn the income. In other words, they were unwilling to sell the property to help the bank mitigate its damages (or their personal damages) and they were unwilling to return the property to the bank, because they wanted to earn income on something that should no longer belong to them. I found this totally disgusting and despicable and would have nothing to do with these people once I discovered it.

The point of highlighting these two distressed scenarios is to make a greater point. Negotiation should always be in the spirit of a win-win situation. Very few people sustain themselves in the real estate industry after a couple of win-lose scenarios. The people who were winning at the expense of the bank in my latter scenario ultimately ended up in bankruptcy or even fraud cases. Their tragedy became a disaster.

By contrast, the individual who made an honest attempt to resolve the situation with the bank, followed by a self-preservation approach, found himself in an unimaginable scenario where he not only was released from all of his negative debt, but received a small amount of money at closing as well. Some call this karma. I would call this a win-win situation. It's nothing more and nothing less.

When you approach any party in a real estate transaction with an honest and fair offer, which they reject, it becomes very instructive as to whom you are dealing with. Don't do business with greedy people because you will usually lose.

My short sale client above (similar numbers but not actual numbers given to protect client confidentiality, by the way) quickly discovered he was dealing with an unreasonable bank, which instructed him that it was best to focus on self-preservation. In the end, the bank mitigated their losses and my client saved himself hundreds of thousands of dollars in losses.

Self-righteousness and real estate, combined, will cost you millions over your lifetime.

I see this frequently with real estate agents who believe they are serving their clients best interests. I call this self-righteousness. These sanctimonious individuals believe that their moral opinion and authority is greater than the average. My personal belief is that we all have an equal right to our moral opinion with no one having a superior opinion. Unfortunately, I run into emotional, judgmental, and self-righteous agents on a daily basis. They start many of their sentences of outrage with "I can't believe....." This is loosely translated as "I'm about to judge you..."

I'm reminded of one such scenario which I wrote about in my last book "The Trump in You." This was an agent who clearly had heard me on the radio for many years and felt that I was a bully because I was candid in my dealings. She believed I was too controlling of the transaction without understanding that I was simply serving my client's best interests at their request. As I mentioned earlier in this book, many agents prefer to be well-liked in their real estate community than within their community of clients. I'm the complete opposite.

Here's that passage from my prior book:

I remember a real estate agent in Charleston, South Carolina who once said back to me "God d***it Bryan! Nobody ever stands up to you because they're afraid of you and I'm going to do it now and I'm not putting up with you. You're not gonna bully me." She was upset at me because I put a very nasty, Trump-like post on Facebook regarding her behavior from the prior day and called her by name.

She had requested an appointment to take her clients inside the home that they were buying for an inspection. We already had it under contract with her clients. It was a high-end home owned by a prominent doctor with a very busy life and schedule. She demanded aggressively that I make the inspection happen at a specific time. She called multiple times demanding an answer and confirmation. My client was in surgery most of the day and didn't get home until late that night.
She was abusive of my time and of my clients' personal privacy. I sent a text-message, left a voicemail, and sent an email demanding she not go to the home the next day until I got back to her with approval. She went anyway, early in the morning and woke my clients with two men walking on their roof. My clients

freaked out. I came unglued because of the outright insolence, lack of respect, and lack of regard for personal privacy. I was stunned by this display of ego and disrespectfulness in defiance of someone's personal property.

Being a radio host and a consumer advocate, I turned it into a story about how I felt real estate agents are some of the most disrespectful people in American business. I named her. I called her out. Apparently, no one in her life had ever had the balls to make her look in a mirror and feel some sense of accountability for her egregious, disrespectful, and horrific behavior.

What she had done was clearly illegal, a licensure violation, and could have resulted in someone being shot or killed.

What came next were threats of lawsuits, ethics complaints, and personal attacks - AGAINST ME. The moment you stand up to someone who is accustomed to plowing over everyone else in their life, you will be met with the harshest of reactions and threats. The most common threat to speaking your mind and being truthful is a reaction by others threatening a lawsuit. By finding the 'Trump in You,' lawsuits no longer scare you.

Lawsuits only scare people who are not sure if their convictions and actions are appropriate. Most people have learned to address the threats against them by bullying you and beating you into submission. The request for an apology is usually the first step followed by a threat similar to a lawsuit or ethics complaint (such as in real estate). Most of the time these threats are not followed by action. These losers typically crash and burn as fast as they erupted because they know they have no righteousness in their outrage.

This passage from my prior book illustrates that sometimes you have to negotiate with or against people who are somewhere between totally ridiculous and completely insane. In this scenario, I believe I was dealing with someone who believed that her clients' interests and timing mattered more than my clients' right to determine when someone else could come into their home. Instead of serving her clients' best interest, she infuriated my clients and created a scenario where they no longer trusted anything this buyer offered or said. This agent did not do a good job in any aspect of negotiating for client.

The second point I want to make here is that I did something completely unpredictable. I've already established that most real estate agents care more about their reputation in the industry than their clients' opinion of them. After attempting to professionally manage the situation, it became obvious I was dealing with an idiot. Those two revelations about agents and this individual clearly instructed me that posting this on my Facebook page would produce far more leverage than attempting to be logical and reasonable (which had already failed).

Once the Facebook post went live, people started commenting and sharing it. I knew she was more interested in industry-reputation than being a good agent for her clients. I now had the leverage with her broker to remove her from the transaction and to hold her accountable as my clients demanded. After this, the transaction closed without a hitch and there were no more problems. Once her broker became involved, the Facebook post was deleted.

These are the kinds of fools and idiots that populate the modern real estate industry. They are real estate agents, mortgage brokers, insurance agents, and every other service provider in the space. In most cases they are completely ignorant, unaware of the rules, how they apply, and what to do. When they make mistakes, due to their ignorance, they lash out at those they've harmed. They refuse to admit how incompetent they allow themselves to be. It is neither my job, nor yours as an intelligent homeowner, to protect them or save them from their idiotic selves.

It is our job to protect ourselves from them. In reality, the art of negotiation sometimes involves doing the exact opposite of what people believe you will do.

As you can tell, this book has nothing to do with politics. However, this chapter is about negotiation and I just used a segment from my book "The Trump in You." What I'm about to say is in no way an endorsement or lack thereof of President Trump.

Trump comes from the real estate field, having had incredible success in hundreds of real estate dealings. Like him or not, Trump frequently does the exact opposite of what people expect him to do in a given situation. I generally don't like that style at all. However, it is frequently necessary in order to conduct a real estate transaction, close it unscathed, while having the hopes of profiting in the process.

The agent I referenced earlier was more worried about her own schedule and getting a roof inspection completed than with proper protocol, ethics, respect, and morality. The fact is her clients did not own this home; my clients did. No one has a right to enter someone else's home without expressed permission and an appointment. This agent believed there would be no consequences for violating basic respect. If I had failed to make as big of a deal of this situation as I did, she would have continued to disrespect my clients and put this transaction in further harm's way.

Instead, my unpredictable style of negotiation and accountability removed her from the transaction and injected a broker who was calm, professional, and respectful. The agent still received a $30,000 commission when her buyers closed on the home, and my sellers received top dollar with no further hassle.

Negotiation is not for the faint of heart. You must be willing to say things people are not going to like. I believe in a three-step process with regard to professionalism.
- Step 1: Ask politely and kindly for what you need or desire.
- Step 2: Reiterate your reasonable position along with an implication of consequences for non-compliance.
- Step 3: Firmly stated your positions again along with specific disappointment that your conditions have not been reasonably addressed.

Did I mention the four-step process? I didn't. I rarely get there. However, step four is doing whatever is moral and legal to protect your interests (and your clients'). Step four was the Facebook post with the 'agent on the roof.' It put an immense amount of social pressure on her and brought accountability back to our transaction.

Step four can sometimes be a threat of a specific consequence or action that will be taken if a deadline is not met. One example of this is in the negotiation of a home repair addendum where we represent the buyer. It is not uncommon to find foundation issues that require repair. Sellers or their agents frequently refuse to make these expensive and necessary repairs. It usually sounds like this:
"if you don't take the property, we'll just put it back on the market and sell it to someone else."

While I don't take offense to that statement, I have plenty of experience showing me that most agents intend to put it back on the market while failing to disclose this known latent defect that we discovered. After a few attempts at logic, my usual response is this:

If you put this property back on the market and offer it without disclosing this known latent defect, then you'll be violating state law and license law. If you are suggesting to me that you would rather put it back on the market and attempt to sell it for the same price as my client has offered to pay without repairing it, I don't believe you. Any agent knows that if you disclose this latent defect as part of your marketing, your next offer is likely to be lower. So I'm left to assume you're telling me you plan to put it back on the market without disclosing it. In that case I will make certain to contact the new buyers' agent the minute they are under contract. That said, your best bet is to negotiate with my buyer, as your financial interests go downhill from here. I'm not going to allow you to kick my buyer to the curb and then fail to disclose this issue to the market as a whole thereafter.

Unless the agent is completely ignorant, they realize I've said far more than what the words actually describe. I've put them on notice that to sell the property without disclosing this latent defect is illegal. In fact, if the new buyer enters into a contract and later finds that the seller failed to disclose a known latent defect, then the seller loses a substantial amount of contract negotiation leverage. The seller entered that contract in bad faith because they knowingly made a material misrepresentation of condition.

Instructing them that I'll be watching is huge leverage for my buyer.

I've also reminded the agent, in my negotiation, that disclosing a latent structural defect as part of the marketing effort is likely to scare most buyers. Since my client is already financially and emotionally invested in the property, they are willing to negotiate a repair that many buyers won't. This means they are likely to get more money with our buyer, offering a reasonable repair addendum, than a buyer who has to know of this issue in advance of writing an offer.

In so many words, I've also implied that the only way to escape making the market aware of this latent defect is to repair the property before putting it back on the market. If they plan to repair and put it back on the market, then it makes no sense not to repair it for my client and close quickly.

This is just one of the dozens of scenarios that are involved in negotiating a real estate transaction. Most unintelligent homeowners and nearly all real estate agents focus on marketing as the key component in hiring a professional to help you sell property. Marketing the property is the easiest part of the sales process. Ironically, most real estate agents still get this part totally wrong.

In order to sell property, you have to sell it four times. The first sales process is in marketing and contract negotiation. That is the easiest. The second sales process is with inspection. The inspection tends to be the most difficult part of the process because too many real estate agents and their clients operate with emotion. If no one on the buying side of the transaction is logical or reasonable that is a very difficult psychological negotiation. There is no way to teach the psychology of negotiating inspections. Only experience does that. While this may sound like a sales pitch, I assure you it isn't. The 3% that I make selling a home is usually recouped and/or earned during the inspection negotiation. I'm careful to watch for language that can unwittingly bind my client to doing more work than the bullet points seem to suggest. I always want due diligence periods to end once we negotiate an inspection. If they do not, we have invited the buyer to open up another financial negotiation with us.

The third negotiation is at the point of an appraisal. Most appraisers are deathly afraid of federal regulations that resulted from the Great Recession and Dodd Frank legislation. In essence, if the appraiser is not incredibly conservative on their value and the property later forecloses, they could be liable to the bank suffering a loss. This is a tragic regulation that causes appraisers to frequently undervalue properties.

I find myself negotiating with these appraisers on a frequent basis when the market is rising and having to use my three-step professional process followed by the fourth step of harsh consequences in order to sell my clients properties for actual market value. This is a troubling and sad reality resulting from government interference with the real estate marketplace.

The fourth negotiation in the home-sale process is at or near closing. This usually results from the buyer getting buyers' remorse, the agent's lack of setting proper expectations, or the absolute nightmare of the mortgage-lending process with the 'First National Bank of Hell.' There are a number of ways to negotiate in this scenario.

As the sellers' real estate agent, the most effective way to negotiate is to actually take a teacher's role in the transaction. If I suspect the agent is struggling with their client due to inexperience and not having set proper expectations, it's my duty to help the agent on the buyer side of the transaction. By doing this, I am serving my client's best interest.

Instead of saying, "that's not my job," I make it my job. I realize this agent, unfortunately, works for a broker who is more interested in teaching them how to get paperwork signed to keep them from getting sued than how to actually best serve their clients. Companies with thousands of agents are typically not the best companies for the average consumer. Most of the training and documentation they propose to you are to protect them with little interest in protecting you.

Because of this culture, especially rampant in markets like Atlanta Georgia, most agents don't know how to set expectations with the clients or coach them properly when they become emotionally bothered by the inherent difficulties in a transaction.

Real estate transactions are incredibly difficult. Even the easiest one is usually not something the average consumer can handle without professional help. The average real estate transaction is anything but easy. Usually near closing, the buyer has become overwhelmed with the demands of the transaction, their life, orchestrating a move, and dealing with the 'First National Bank of Hell' and obtaining a mortgage.

Sometimes it's as simple as assuring the buyer they are not alone, this is not uncommon, and that everything is going to be okay. In these very tedious moments, I try my best to work with the other agent to give them all the ammunition possible to get the clients comfortably to closing and my clients' home sold for top dollar.

In other words, my marketing and presentation may be anything but humble, but humility must be injected at the most critical moments or deals frequently unravel.

12 HOMEOWNERS' ASSOCIATIONS

It just wouldn't be right for me to write a real estate book and not include this chapter. For the entirety of my real estate career I have been fighting the political entities known as homeowners' associations.

The origination of the modern homeowners' association was for a legitimate reason. These were developed to maintain the values and integrity of the neighborhood and to prevent homeowners from turning their homes into eyesores, running businesses in their front yard, endangering neighbors, or otherwise ruining adjacent properties' values. That's it! Homeowners' associations are to maintain value.

Unfortunately, homeowners' associations in the last two decades have evolved into something much more than that. They have evolved into a way for developers to make residual income and exert infinite control over buyers and homeowners.

I was recently contacted by a homeowners' association in which my family has property. Our property is not for sale. Legally, I'm not the owner. My wife is. I have set up a simple online marketing sales website for the community. Our goal with this site is to meet buyers interested in the development. I took videos and pictures and used some non-copyrighted material along with a Google ad words campaign to drive traffic from interested parties. I received a call from someone on behalf of the developer who stated, "this is a big problem." Obviously, they were threatened because my marketing site was above theirs on Google.

In an effort to convince me to take down my marketing, they pointed to a provision in the covenants and restrictions that prohibit owners in the community from using the name of the community in any marketing. It works, I can't live in 'Atlanta Springs' (fake name) as an owner, subject to the covenants and restrictions legally, and call my business Atlanta Springs Realty. I understand the spirit as there is a legitimate concern of public confusion.

That was not the case in the scenario I'm explaining here. They simply were attempting to eliminate competition (which was actually promoting their community making this even more insane) by manipulating the spirit of the covenants and restrictions in order to exert control and leverage over an owner. Fortunately, I'm not the idiot they thought I was.

Disingenuously, I thanked them for the phone call and pointed out that I do not own a property in the community. My wife owns the property. I then asked them if they would have a problem if Coldwell Banker were to set up a sales site in the same way. I specifically asked "would you really alienate [potentially] several hundred real estate agents by making this phone call to them? It's rather insulting quite frankly!"

It was explained to me that this is different because my wife does own the property and we are advertising the community. I reminded them again that my wife owns the property in the community. I don't. I then dropped the bombshell: I own the real estate company, not my wife. Therefore they had no power or influence over me or my company whatsoever.

I was then asked if I was willing to take down the site. I said "no" and I told this person "you can tell the developer's principles that I think they are ridiculous and petty."

The HOA, which is controlled by the developer, as they sell the neighborhood, attempted to bully me into not selling property in the community. The point here is that they used the covenants and restrictions to try to exert this power.

It's very sad that these situations ever occur in this industry. I've developed a nice website for this community where my family owns a second home. This is a common practice for real estate companies, especially for communities where potential buyers frequently search. It's absolutely normal what I'm doing. And it's very clear that we don't represent the development and are seeking buyers to represent. There is no public confusion; at least that a judge would conclude.

I'm telling you this story because it illustrates my hypothesis that the modern-day homeowners' association, with its modern rules, is more about controlling homeowners that protecting value.

In my state of Georgia, roughly one in five homeowners live in a homeowners' association. That's 2 million people. These numbers ring true throughout most of the country.

In my primary residence, a high-rise condo building in Buckhead, I recently became aware of some grievances by other owners in the building. Given my vast experience dealing with homeowners' associations hundreds of times, something struck me as bizarre, so I sought the advice of an expert manager of homeowners' associations.

In this discussion with an expert, I was led to an individual who informed me that my specific building had turned down a large settlement offer for a government transportation project a few years earlier. I was shown a proposed settlement that we didn't take. The situation was so bizarre that I couldn't shake the thoughts or questions out of my head for the entire day. I simply couldn't understand why someone on our board of directors would stomp on an opportunity to receive a free six-figure settlement. After all, we weren't even suing them at that point and were still being given the opportunity to take a settlement.

The only conclusion I could surmise was that someone was afraid that entering into that settlement process could in fact open up a legitimate court ordered discovery into our board of directors for the homeowners' association. I was onto something.

As of this writing, I still don't know the true reason we turned down free money. What I do know is that I found out that the settlement resulted from a transportation partnership with the master developer of our community. One of their developer partners was the builder who constructed our community. That builder placed the individual who stopped the free money on the board of directors. Unless we change our bylaws, he has a lifetime appointment with limited ability to remove him.

Does this make sense? If it doesn't, it proves my point even more. What I just described is so convoluted and so complex that the average homeowner will never take five seconds attempting to figure it out. If you do understand what I just described, it appears to be a significant conflict of interest. The truth, absent a big lawsuit, is not discoverable.

As a result of these findings, I attended a meeting of our homeowners' association's board of directors. I brought this and other points that I found concerning regarding the lack of transparency in our building. I demanded answers within 30 days. Within that timeframe, I received a letter from our homeowners' association's attorney basically telling me to 'get lost' and that 'they don't have to.'

As an owner in another similar homeowners' association in Atlanta, I was able to request and see the same level of data almost instantly when I requested it there. However, in my primary residence the homeowners' association denied me out right. Whether they are hiding something or not is yet to be determined.

What I discovered in this process is that our homeowners' fees and overall building revenue are not acceptably in line with a very similar but older building with fewer condominium units. At a minimum, this points to mismanagement of our homeowners' association because of a lack of accountability for our board of directors and specifically the appointee I described above. Since he never comes up for election, the average homeowner doesn't realize he's operating with a lifetime appointment. This is not right.

Let me take a departure for a moment. My experience with homeowners' associations in recent years, including the scenarios described above, strike me as a cultural phenomenon we are all experiencing at every level of our lives. For decades Washington DC has operated in this way.

Whether you are a Republican, Democrat, or unaffiliated most Americans agree that Washington DC is broken and fails to represent our interests as American voters. I find very few people of any political persuasion that disagree with that statement. Regretfully and sadly, even our homeowners' associations have taken to this culture of Washington DC politics. Generally, they are power-hungry board members who serve their own interests (or that of special interests) and ignore the will of the majority of the people. This is happening in our churches, in our communities, in local politics, at our workplaces, and certainly in Washington DC.

As a result of this, barring any significant regression back to past standards, I plan to eventually escape ownership of anything in a homeowners' association.

Even rental properties present significant challenges with homeowners' associations. I recently received a letter from a community that has $90,000 townhomes in it. It informed me that my water hose was not coiled properly beside the home. I posted this on Facebook and it literally went viral. Almost no one agreed with the letter. The most negative responses I received directed at me were centered on the stupidity of owning a property with a homeowners' association in the first place. It's hard to disagree with those people isn't it?

Recently, for another rental property, I received $800 worth of fines and late fees over a dent in a gutter, of which I was never notified. In fact, as the situation escalated over the course of three months, I sent three letters asking for statements to which they never responded. Gone are the days of protecting the integrity of the community. After a very harsh and threatening battle, I settled the $800 in charges by allowing them to rob me of $150 instead. I have paid all of my dues otherwise.

You may not realize it but a substantial amount of profit earned by property management companies is not management fees but fines and late-fee penalties. These companies are not interested in the way the community looks. They are trying to improve the way their bank account looks at your expense. Unfortunately, most owners underwrite this behavior by doing nothing or saying nothing about it.

Now, back to where I live. I love the building and most of the people that live there. I've never been around a group of neighbors that actually communicate the way we do.

Recently, one of my neighbors (who I know well) had his unit broken into by the property manager. You didn't misread that statement. As a handicapped individual who was renovating his condo, I believe he had some infraction as to how he obtained approvals to do renovations. Notwithstanding that possibility, the property manager believed this resident had thrown ceramic tile down the trash chute. If that's true, and can be proven, he certainly deserves to be fined and pay for any damage that might have occurred. Those were the allegations. However, I'm not aware of the truth.

What I do know is that the property manager made an egregious mistake. This mistake is so significant that I believe it's a rare insight into the truth behind how these people actually behave when managing our communities. This person was filling in after our manager was fired. Apparently, she was the director of the managers for the high-rises they manage in metro Atlanta. Arrogance eventually catches up to everyone. Without a doubt, this manager was incredibly arrogant.

Believing she was about the catch my neighbor, she called him one morning and woke him up. She demanded he come to the management office. I guess for now we're back in high school according to her, right? Time to go to the principal's office for bad behavior!

He refused.

After his refusal he went back to sleep. She visited his condo unit and began knocking on his door and ringing his doorbell. Idiotically, she began showing her true colors not realizing that this handicapped individual was the only person in our building with a Ring doorbell. The one that immediately starts taking videos when motion activates it!

All of this was caught on camera. She's yelling at him, demanding he opened the door, and calling this trash chute issue an emergency. Her body language, stance, and overall demeanor were extremely aggressive, dismissive, and abusive. Even worse, she obtained a key and entered his unit.

Before presenting this video to the community, I had posted another video from the same doorbell showing the current manager sniffing and listening into various units. Most of my neighbors were horrified by the simple photographs. The Facebook post said that this particular management company is spying on residents and entering units. Knowing they would defend such a statement by denying that they actually entered units, I withheld the video of the break-in by the manager.

Sure enough! They provided the innocent response that they never enter units, don't have access to the keys, and were simply sniffing for smokers. Sounds totally benign doesn't it?

Boom! Enter the video of the manager getting the key and entering the unit while a homeowner is sleeping.

If you find all of this troubling and disgusting, you are not alone. Most intelligent homeowners believe that homeowners' association managers are not protecting their best interests and truly preserving the values in the community. Having to go public with such behavior in order to hold management accountable is damaging to the community.

Some of our residents were not happy that local NBC affiliate "11 Alive" picked up the story and ran it as the lead story on the six o'clock news. I was ecstatic. This rare homeowner leverage held the property managers accountable.

It is far more important for homeowners' associations to operate with care, diligence, and integrity than for communities to endure short-term embarrassment stemming from the actions of a bad management company, board of directors, or other illicit activity. Allowing such behavior to continue, without accountability, destroys the financial balance sheets and values of communities.

Getting on the board of directors of these communities typically is just like Washington DC politics. As of the writing of this book, my wife has been on the board of directors in our community for a few months. She was recruited by 50 homeowners because she has been a successful and effective sales agent in the building and demonstrated exceptional leadership and judgment. She was overwhelmingly elected as a director by the community's residents. Because of the internal politics of the board and some of the dynamics explained herein, she feels it has been quite a waste of time.

Just like Washington DC, good-natured honorable people get elected to serve their community and their interests only to get eaten alive once they reach the political meat grinder in our nation's capital. Homeowners' associations are simply a microcosm of that same disgusting phenomenon.

The best leadership you can offer your homeowners' association is to be a voice and a proxy of the common interest of the community. I recently conducted a homeowner satisfaction survey of my high-rise community described above. The building's management and manager (the latter in place just four months) had an approval rating below 50%. Rumor has it that management and our board of directors are troubled by the fact that "someone" did an unofficial survey of the residence.

The survey found that most of my grievances were consistently echoed by the majority of the respondents. Sending a random survey to dozens of people and getting a 30% response rate is unprecedented. I plan to use that survey to illustrate to the homeowners that what most of us believe and think (which is in direct contrast with management's money making activities) is commonly held opinion in the building.

The entrepreneurial homeowner likely is not a good candidate for a homeowners' association. A compliance officer at a bank probably makes the perfect resident in the modern homeowners' association. Before buying in these communities, you should thoroughly review what other people have experienced there. If it's an investment, you should determine if it makes sense given the fact that you will become more of a target for the board of directors and the management company as a landlord. Some of them outright see you as an opportunity to add more money to their bottom line. Others self-righteously punish you for investing into the community and having tenants.

As a resident, you have to ask yourself if you can handle getting a letter on Wednesday that your JetSki was in the driveway at 10 AM the day after Memorial Day, that your trashcan wasn't hidden completely from view, or that you didn't properly coil your hosepipe. These aren't compliance issues driven toward maintaining the integrity of the community. They are legal steps with the intent of fining you and generating more income.

I believe in the spirit of homeowners' associations entirely. The building is non-smoking, meaning there should be no smoking inside the building. If I live in a housing community, pink flamingos, purple houses, and cars on blocks in the front yard should be aggressively handled.

I don't believe a single homeowners' association was ever designed in the spirit of worrying about how a hose pipe is coiled by the spigot. That is where I draw the line!

13 PAYING OFF YOUR PRIMARY HOME

As we near the end of the "The Intelligent Homeowner,' I felt it necessary to tackle perhaps the biggest struggle I have had in my financial life. That struggle is whether or not to pay off a primary residence.

On the surface, it makes complete sense. Owning your home 'free and clear' is a financial achievement that very few people make until very late in life. However, there are some examples where that is not the best idea.

When we sold our home in South Carolina to move to Georgia, we had substantial equity. The intention was to pay off our condo and live mortgage free. It's an attractive proposition, but it lacks a certain pressure that I find to be healthy in my life.

Having some payments to make and some financial pressure, tends to drive me much harder. As a result, I stay more focused because there is a risk to do otherwise. With the principle in mind that I can afford 25% of my household income in a mortgage payment, my risks of having a mortgage are greatly mitigated as compared to most Americans.

Instead of paying off a $350,000 mortgage which has a 4.25% interest rate, we decided to invest in a property with a 13 to 16% return. This means just $150,000 of the money we would expect to pay off the mortgage is now producing enough income to cover the entire payment. Those properties have no mortgage. The difference between our primary payoff and what is needed to cover the payment is now invested into income producing properties which produce additional income for our family.

As sophisticated and experienced real estate investors, we were qualified to do the opposite of what most of the financial coaching books advise. We took some risk on a primary residence, although very mitigated, and then invested the money into investment-grade real estate.

What is investment-grade real estate? It's anything that makes a great rental property with a double-digit return (net operating income) on your money.

Here's my rules on paying off real estate. It makes no sense in my prime earning years to pay off my primary residence unless the interest rate is approaching or into the double digits. At double-digit interest rates the risk reward scenario changes in favor of paying off my primary residence. At 4 to 5% rates, and with my primary mortgage payment being less than 25% of my gross monthly income, I'm better off using my cash to invest in income producing property.

On the lower end of the market, a 40-year-old can buy one property per year until they're 65 and earn a net income of $12-$15,000 (unadjusted for inflation meaning in today's money) per month. For the average person, this is more than enough to retire and retain your lifestyle. This doesn't include 401(k)s, stock, pensions, IRAs, or other investments that pay monthly income. This is mortgage-free real estate.

At the point of retirement, or nearing retirement, I do think it makes sense to pay off your primary residence. Usually, the preretirement residence is bigger and more expensive that what is needed in retirement. Frequently, if you don't use your home as a piggy bank taking out loans and cash-out refinances over this period, you'll pay it off naturally anyway.

At a minimum level, I believe that real estate investments, free of mortgages are a better retirement planning strategy that even an IRA or 401(k). In fact, I stopped funding our IRAs because I can produce much higher, consistent returns in real estate than having cash stuck inside of the government regulated fund with their huge penalties for withdrawal prior to retirement.

I do think that for everyone who has employer matching on a 401(k) plan should take every cent available (in employer match) since that is free money. I do not believe that a no-IRA, no-401(k) strategy is appropriate for everyone. If you are more risk averse then diversity of assets can be psychologically beneficial. After all, the point of financial freedom is to reduce or eliminate stress.

Notwithstanding these thoughts, paying off your mortgage is an accomplishment that is best executed when you plan to retire or shift your focus to a semi-retirement status. Contrary to what many financial experts recommend, your best action during prime earning years is to:

- Invest everything allowable in your 401(k) where your employer will match your contribution. Take the free money! No real estate return will eclipse a 50 or 100% match of up to 3% of your income or more.
- Keep a mortgage payment on your primary residence that is less than 25% of your gross household monthly income. After creating a three to six month emergency fund, in the case of job

loss or crisis, invest 25% of your monthly income that remains into income-producing real estate. This means you have to pay taxes and live on 50% of your gross monthly income. Most Americans are far from that and that's why they struggle.

- Depending on your age, develop a strategy with your primary home mortgage that will pay it off the year you plan to retire. If you are already 55, for instance, and still have 27 years left on your mortgage, don't fret. An original mortgage of $300,000 at 4.25% can be paid off in 10 to 12 years with an extra $1200 per month in principal payments. If you cannot simultaneously make this additional payment and save money to invest in real estate, then it is advisable to reduce your primary residence-costs by selling this one and buying something less expensive (at the next opportunity where the market needs sellers ONLY). Most people are unwilling to make these sorts of sacrifices and thus trade their retirement lifestyle for present luxuries.
- It's helpful to coordinate all of these goals between your financial advisor, your preferred real estate expert, and your accountant because each situation is different. The likely disagreement of these multiple professionals will also provide enlightenment that most people are unwilling to seek.

After your prime earning years, your main objective is to enjoy your life and lifestyle without financial worries. This means your primary residence should be debt free. If you are unable to make the additional $1200 per month during your prime earning years I outlined above then you will have to accept a smaller home in retirement. Let's say you can only make additional payments of $600 per month for the next 10-12 years. Your present value $300,000 home will have a remaining mortgage of $162,000 instead of the $238,000 balance had you made the fixed mortgage payment.

With reasonable appreciation, in a decade, this home should be worth $400,000 to $500,000, maybe more. If the market is soft and it doesn't make sense to sell it, most people would simply refinance it extending their payments out another 30 years and greatly reducing their monthly outlay so they could proceed with their retirement. This is why I recommend correcting this issue now by buying a home that fits your minimum current needs and can be paid in full by retirement. Reaching retirement in 10 to 12 years, still making a payment on an original $300,000 mortgage, during a market collapse is not a healthy scenario unless your retirement income can afford the continued payment.

Obviously, these scenarios are the types of situations that cause most of us to say "I wish I was 30 again." A 30-year-old with two great household incomes can buy a home now on a 30-year mortgage and never look back. Their problem is the propensity to keep upgrading into bigger and more luxurious homes as their income rises. Obviously, this is not a bad thing so long as you continue to reduce your mortgage amortization as you climb the luxury-housing ladder.

This means that your first home can be a 30-year mortgage, and you will not have to make additional payments in order to pay it off by retirement at the age of 60. However, if your household income doubles in a decade and you're looking for the McMansion in the suburbs, I can endorse that move so long as your new mortgage is less than 25% of your household income and is on a 15 to 20 year amortization schedule. To do otherwise is potentially financial suicide. You cannot predict the future!

If after reading this book you have decided you do not have the pain and risk tolerance to own investment real estate (where some tenant doesn't pay the rent or destroys the interior), then your only other real estate mechanism for financial freedom is aggressively paying down your primary-home mortgage as rapidly as possible.

14 CONCLUSION

This book was designed for my clients and customers. I plan to write an investment book at some point in the future. I've outlined some of the scams and frauds that populate the housing industry. I've warned you about the unfortunate lack of professionalism and competence that is at every level of the housing industry. I've given you many secrets of the real estate brokerage profession, so that you can defend yourself against the housing sharks that make up the vast majority of so-called professionals.

I've given you more free investment advice than any $5-10,000 seminar will ever impart. The main goal of those real estate seminars is to get you to buy their monthly coaching series which is thousands of dollars that you ultimately could use toward your savings and real estate investments.

So long as I can collect a referral fee from the agent you use in whichever market you choose to purchase, sell, or invest (in the world), your $10,000 seminar is unneeded and a monthly coaching fee I will not charge. If you are buying, selling, or investing in Metro Atlanta, then you get to tap into all of my knowledge you need in every situation and transaction, for your benefit.

Considering that most of my competitors charge 5 to 7%, most of which have virtually no experience, you are paying me an 'average' fee for well above average service and unprecedented coaching. If you're a buyer or in another market, you pay me no fee at all, since I refer you to the best agent!

If you need assistance in buying a property that isn't listed, I do that as well for a reasonable fee resulting from the required scope of services.

If your 'brother's cousin's younger sister' just got her license and you feel obligated to help her out, but realize she knows very little, I can advise you before you hire her as your agent.

I would point out that you really not helping your 'brother's cousin's younger sister' by giving her the business to 'help her out' because you're not teaching her how to earn the business. You're teaching her how to be entitled to the business. I have seen people with one and two million-dollar homes list with relatives or friends that are new or relatively inexperienced in the business.

If you were at risk of having a heart attack and quadruple bypass surgery, would you want a 29-year-old relative who just finished residency to perform your surgery or an older, tenured doctor who's performed thousands of such surgeries?

You would obviously not want to have a serious medical problem addressed by an inexperienced doctor. Why would you want to have a financial heart attack by using an inexperienced agent on your most valuable financial asset? The best way to honor a relative who is not yet experienced enough to handle your real estate transactions is to ask an agent like me if we would honor their license with a referral fee in order to obtain the business and accomplish those goals at the same time (re: 'helping' a relative and making the best financial decisions).

The biggest mistakes the unintelligent homeowner make are skipping the most laborious and important parts of the housing process. When most people decide to sell, they are ready to get it on the market yesterday. When they want to buy they want to point and click and close in a matter of days. Sometimes, the painful nature of interviewing agents, asking tough questions, and vetting your decisions (while not attractive in terms of time economy) is the front-loaded hard work required to make the most money in your housing transactions.

Let's say you read this book and you're overwhelmingly convinced that I should be your next real estate agent. I agree with you, wholeheartedly! However, that doesn't mean that I believe you deserve any less of a presentation or initial consultation than I give a potential client in a very competitive situation. To deny that experience, would eliminate my ability to set proper expectations and to coach you on how to make the best determinations as you move forward.

Remember, I told you early in this book that you make your money when you buy not when you sell. The reason for that absolute truth is because the due diligence along with your overall research and discovery make you an expert on that particular microcosm of the marketplace. After all, you are investing six figures or more of your own money into an asset. The process of such vetting is a lot of front-loaded work. At times, you have to do all the work to make a purchase on several properties only to finally purchase one of them.

The reason I say "you make your money when you buy" is because you've done a whole lot of work on several properties in order to only purchase one of them. This means you turned down several properties that the average unintelligent homeowner would have purchased in haste that would end up being bad deals in the long run.

Because of your extra effort on the front end, you avoided those unattractive purchases and instead bought the one that was the most appealing for your financial goals.

Hiring professional advisors is exactly the same. It's not easy and frequently you must have multiple experiences before you meet someone like me or even encounter an instructive book like this (whether you hire me or not).

Having learned the hard way, before I hire a new member of our real estate team, I review their resume, having rejected most of the candidates at this point, and then ask them to take a personality profile. Without revealing our proprietary approach, we are looking for specific personality profiles resulting from the tests that we use.

After matching the criteria for these two steps, we meet with the prospect in person and conduct a series of 'gotcha' questions to determine if the prospect is a good fit. I would list the questions here but then I'd have to change them making them irrelevant. If they pass that process, then they meet with "corporate."

What is "corporate?" Every man who is married has "corporate." It's called my wife. The relevance here is that she is my soulmate and my business partner. In order for us to make a hire, the recruit has to pass with flying colors on all of these steps. If they don't, we simply can't hire them. Obviously, we're not hiring very many people. We are looking for a few people who are absolutely the best.

In your financial life, you are looking for one person in each sector that can be your advocate, coach, and partner in their area of expertise.

When you are hiring a real estate or financial expert, it's best to have you and "corporate" at the same meeting. Here are the kinds of questions (although in no way limited to these) I would ask a real estate professional that I am considering hiring to list my home:

- What do you think of my neighborhood?
- What is the worst feature of my home?
- Have you worked with a client like me in the past?
- Regardless of market value, what you think the first buyer will offer on this home?
- How many homes did you sell personally (not your team) in the past year?
- Do you currently own your own home or rent?
- Before becoming an agent, tell me about the first home buying or selling experience you had with another real estate agent and what you disliked most about it. Also tell me why you got into real estate.
- Tell me about the last real estate training session that you attended. Who gave it and what was the subject?
- How long have you held your real estate license?

There are plenty of questions like these I could suggest. However, let me take these questions again and tell you what we are attempting to discover:

- What do you think of my neighborhood? *This is a 'gotcha' question. This agent better tell me something really great as the first words out of their mouths as a reaction to this question or I'm not hiring them. If the agents first thought isn't to point out the most exciting feature they don't understand marketing because you've just given them a secret question (in 'gotcha' style) to prove it to you. You don't have to agree with the feature they suggest, but it better be one big positive statement. Now, after an opening statement is positive, don't judge them after that.*

- What is the worst feature of my home? *This better be an honest answer because it's a 'gotcha' question. Be prepared for something pretty negative. The question is pretty specific. You asked for the worst feature of the home so you should expect something pretty negative. If they can't find one thing wrong with your home this is the first indication that everything they've said in their pitch is BS.*

- Have you worked with a client like me in the past? *This question is a landmine and would scare the heck out of me! What you are looking for here is nothing more and nothing less than honesty. The appropriate response would be to ask "what do you mean?" My suggestion to you is to reiterate the question verbatim. Within five minutes, real estate agents have already formed an opinion of the prospect they are pitching. The type of person that would read this book and actually ask that question is probably someone that is not easily confused or fooled. My personal answer might be something like "I can tell you're the kind of person that's not going to tolerate apathy or a lack of accountability. I find those clients to be the best clients for me because they are very candid and expect me to be the same." There is no right or wrong answer here. It's a way to solicit a statement from this agent that is not canned BS. A great agent can quickly answer this question without a problem and 'BS artist' will fall over themselves (because most of their rhetoric is canned and practiced).*

- Regardless of market value, what do you think the first buyer will offer on this home? *In this question I'm looking for the truth. Most real estate agents do something called "bidding for the listing." I lose many listings by refusing to do this. "Bidding for the listing" is the process of telling the seller a number that is remotely believable (but highly unlikely) in an attempt to win the listing. Unless the market is collapsing, the number given to this question should be within 2 to 3% of the suggested list price they stated. Usually, agents tell sellers numbers that are too good to be true only to beat them up on price three to four weeks into the listing. I hear this frequently from home sellers whose listing contract expired from the multiple listing service when their agent failed to sell the home. Many sellers believe that listing with the agent confident they can get the highest price will somehow impact the final sales value. This is totally untrue. Sometimes, the agent with the lowest value is the one attempting to be the most honest in a sea of agents who are either ignorant or lying.*

- How many homes did you sell personally (not your team) in the past year? *This is a question I would suggest asking over the telephone before you meet with the agent. If you are interviewing multiple agents one of the other agents could answer this question for you to see if the prospect told you the truth. Understand, that some people sell homes and their success gets reported under a main team member just as in our situation. Generally, agents with a great deal of listing and sales experience have their own website (not a subdomain of their company) and show some evidence online of sales in the hemisphere of what they reported to you.*

- Do you currently own your own home or rent? *Someone who does not presently own their own home is not the real estate listing agent for you. They should be someone who is working with first-time buyers helping them convert from renting to homeownership. Trusting this person to help you sell a home (when they don't even own one) means that their lifestyle and understanding is not conducive in most cases to seller marketing.*

- Before becoming an agent, tell me about the first home buying or selling experience you had with another real estate agent and what you dislike most about it. Also tell me why you got into real estate. *As I described in an earlier chapter, most real estate agents are notorious for saying "I love working with people and that's why I'm in the real estate business." Others will say that they love one thing or the other about helping people, overcoming challenges etc. All of this is BS! Every real estate agent got into this business for the purpose of making more money than they thought possible in any other career. We are a bunch of egomaniacal, self-serving salespeople. There are two of us: those that want to help you while we make a ton of money and those that don't care about you at all and want to make a ton of money. If the answer to this question is anything other than money and freedom, it's a lie! Here's how I would answer that question in both parts: "I got into this business because I was so displeased with how I was treated in my first couple of real estate transactions as a young adult. I realized that even these experienced agents were not capable of serving my needs as well as I could do if I got my license. At the same time, I was a full-time media host and was disgusted with how I was being treated. I knew, if I had some control over my goals, I could do exceptionally well and that has proven to be true. The main reason I got into this business was freedom from a corporation so that I can control my own experience." I learned this while recruiting real estate agents over many years. After a few hundred of them, I noticed a consistency in the freedom category. When agents got into this business because of an entrepreneurial spirit and a desire for personal freedom, they usually did far better than those who say "I just like working with people." That latter phrase is a disingenuous way of saying I feel bad that I'm doing this for freedom and money. This means they are ashamed of their potential success. In light of that, how can they bring you success if they can't even be proud of their own desire to create personal success?*

- Tell me about the last real estate training session that you attended. Who gave it and what was the subject? *This is another 'gotcha' question. As a seller of real estate, I want to know if they are engaged in "screw me compliance training" or in sales training that helps me as a seller get more money for my home. I call it "screw me compliance training" because most companies now teach agents how to get you to sign documents to release liability away from them and place it on you. If their answer to this question is anything other than "how to use [some] digital technology to produce more business, more showings, and more sales" than they clearly don't know what training is. If I had just sat through 30 hours of continuing education as required by the state of Georgia, I would not answer your question by describing that boring process. That is not training.*

That is continuing education as required by the bureaucracy of our government. Training is something that will help me be better at what I do. Usually, big real estate companies don't give true training. Training is when I attend an event to learn how to be uniquely better than my competition. For instance, my wife and I travel two or three times per year to agent seminars across the country where we share ideas that work.

- How long have you held your real estate license? *Believe it or not, this is a big question. Most real estate agents have limited experience. I would ask them this question over the phone before the appointment. Let's say you asked me this question. My answer would be "19years." You would then go to the Georgia real estate commission website and discover that I've only been licensed for roughly 9 years. You should hit me with that early in our meeting. My reply would be that I have been licensed in Georgia since my application in 2009 and I started my real estate career in 1999 with a license in South Carolina. The point of this question is that some agents will tell you they've been in real estate 'sales' for 10 years. Translation: they've been in some form of sales for 10 years and got their license a few months ago. This is the canary in the coal mine that much of the presentation could be disingenuous.*

These sorts of questions throw scam artists for a loop. Most sellers ask the same exact questions, which are anything but these kinds of questions and therefore the answers from agents are predictable. These agents are the perfect chameleons who will steal your equity due to their incompetence.

If they stumble all over themselves in these sort of questions, then they will have no idea to deal with the dozens of problems that will present themselves in your transaction nor how to overcome the four negotiating steps necessary to get your home sold.

In order to sell your home for the most money, in the least amount of time, and with the fewest hassles you should expect to pay somewhere between 5 to 7% in commission (while there is no standard fee) while hiring an agent who's been in the industry for no less than five years, having sold at least 20 listings in the past 12 months and no fewer than 100 sales during their career.

Do yourself a favor and do not allow the agent you are thinking about hiring to know these are your criteria. If they do not meet them, do not hire them. Why would you hire someone with less than five years of experience who hasn't accomplished what you're asking them to do dozens of times already?

The biggest challenge that American homeowners have is being too nice to the real estate community. We don't deserve it!

Our industry is out to steal your equity and convert it into commission. You might as well have the most experienced and accomplished people in the face of that potential reality.

Most real estate agents who sell dozens of homes per year and have a decade or more of tenure in this industry, are not what I'm describing in this book. It's hard to make it in real estate sales for a long period of time if you mistreat the lifeblood of your business: clients.

The problem is usually in the population of agents with less than five years of experience who are lying about most everything they are presenting. They are very good at convincing you they are one of "the experienced folks."

Since I have well over 30,000 hours of experience in this industry, I rarely lose even against the most experienced agents and typically win the business of a new client in a competitive situation. It's usually these inexperienced agents with a limited number of sales and a book full of lies that make me the victim of a failed presentation where I don't earn the business. Sometimes the scammy sales pitch is just too good to pass (until it costs you major equity in the sale or your home doesn't sell at all).

I've always said that the biggest threat to the best agents are the lying ones. After all, I presented a reality of real estate in this book that is complex, deviant, and overly regulated and where most everything in some way is difficult.

It's easy for someone to drive to your home in daddy's six-figure sports car with their one nice suit, an expensive presentation assembled by an office manager, give a canned presentation (while promising the world and a sales price from a different universe), and defeat an agent trying to tell you the truth.

Regrettably, throughout my career, I have met thousands of unintelligent homeowners. They have been scammed and screwed by this industry because they were unaware of just how greedy it can be. Most who struggle use emotions over logic. I've also had the pleasure of meeting and working with thousands of intelligent homeowners. From those contrasting experiences, I developed the content of this book over two decades.

This book is dedicated to the consumer, the intelligent homeowner, and now to you. You are now more informed about our industry than 95% of the so-called sales-professionals.

Go forth, get rich, do it honestly, and make more money from real estate than you ever thought possible.

If you need my help, you know the drill! therealestateexperts.com
bryan@housedog.com

ABOUT THE AUTHOR

Bryan Crabtree is married to Mackenzie Crabtree. Together they are the "Crabtree Team" in metro-Atlanta. Mackenzie operates an REO brokerage in Georgia and South Carolina under TheRealEstateExperts.com banner.

Bryan bought his first house when he was 19. He's bought and sold nearly 200 personal homes and represented over 5,000 clients as a broker. During the financial crash he saved nearly 500 homeowners from foreclosure by negotiating with banks (along with legal partners) on their behalf.

By the time he was 30, he had developed a seven office real estate company with a major national franchise which had 408 agents, nearly 40 employees, and operated in two states. He sold it in 2008, just before the height of the financial crash.

After a brief stint in management, he went back into sales forming the Crabtree Team with his wife. They were the number one agents in Charleston, SC metro for three years. In 2009, they also opened TheRealEstateExperts.com in metro-Atlanta where they are now one of the most accomplished sales teams.

"My top priorities are to overcome obstacles and assist clients with achieving their real estate goals with the least hassle," adds Crabtree. His experience in handling client's resale needs and corporate properties, enhances his attention to detail and service to consumers. Bryan Crabtree says, "I am meticulous about following-up and following-through on the commitments I make. I'm dedicated to giving my clients a truly exceptional experience. Communication is key!"

Bryan is one of the few brokers in Georgia who have previously taken the Certified Relocation Professional and Global Mobility Specialist training as given by the Employment Relocation Council.

Bryan is a regular expert analyst on business, real estate, and politics on WSB Radio, Salem Media Group, RT and dozens of other radio and television outlets throughout America and the world.

You can find his sales and content sites at therealestateexperts.com, myatlantahomelistings.com, househuntingonline.com (home evaluation), and talk40.com (business, news, politics, real estate).

www.ingramcontent.com/pod-product-compliance
Lightning Source LLC
Chambersburg PA
CBHW020435220526
45464CB00002B/710